INDIANS, ANIMALS, SPIRITS

MY 12 YEARS WITH THE LAKOTA SIOUX AT PINE RIDGE

LIVING, LEARNING, HELPING, TEACHING

ISBN # 978-0-578-57558-2
COPYRIGHT WORLDWIDE RIGHTS PROTECTED
RALPH SCHULTZ
ALBUQUERQUE NEW MEXICO USA
AUGUST 31, 2019

2

BIOGRAPHY

I was born and lived on Chicago's South Side from 1947-1957 and then in Evergreen Park where I graduated from High School in 1965, a Chicago Southwest suburb. Then I went to Northwestern University in Evanston, Illinois where I graduated in 1969 with a honors major in history. I received a Master of Business degree in finance and economics in 1972. I worked for 35 years in the investment business as a corporate bond specialist and in equipment leasing and structured finance for international banks in Chicago including as a vice-president for Deutsche Bank, the leading bank in Germany. I switched to teaching in 2003 and worked at tribal colleges from 2005-2009 at the Pine Ridge Indian Reservation in South Dakota and the Navajo Reservation in Arizona. For the past nine since 2009 I have been an adjunct economics instructor at Central New Mexico Community College. In 1968 I went to Moscow Russia, the Soviet Union, to study Russian language and culture with a USA college group. I was a strategic intelligence analyst in the United States Army. I traveled to Pine Ridge many times from 1996-2008.

RALPH SCHULTZ   ECONOMICS PROFESSOR NEW MEXICO USA

Email: ralphpineridge77@ GMAIL.COM

INTRODUCTION

This book is a compilation of my experiences and friends from 1996-2008 at the Pine Ridge Indian reservation in western South Dakota, the Black Hills, and the Navajo Reservation in Arizona in 2009. It was quite a journey and the book cannot fully explain what I encountered and felt inside. It was a transformative experience. I am so happy I had this time with the Indians and as accepted by them. The two pictures of Chicago represent the powerful advanced USA society developed from Native American land and natural resources at no financial cost or payment.

The first section is about animals. My experiences follow with some spiritual commentary at the end. So enjoy and learn !!

Acknowledgements

I would also like to thank Merrilyn Sweet, my high school classmate, who voluntarily assisted me to transcribe my oral recordings and provided some helpful ideas. She resides in Riverside, Illinois, a beautiful suburb with many parks and trees and well maintained older classical homes. And two designed by Frank Lloyd Wright, the famous architect. Thank you Merrillyn.

And to Blaine, my 29-year-old son. Thank you for helping me managing photographs and getting it published and marketed on social media.

Kurt Tyler helped me with the book covers. He has two books out on Amazon. One discusses opinions about race. Very interesting.

TABLE of CONTENTS

THE STORY----SECTION

NOTE: I did my own editing which was a long arduous process. You will see a few imperfections. Hey, I am imperfect and so are people and the world. I think the book is attractive, and very readable with many great photos. And I am honest about myself and my thoughts, beliefs.

In the Lakota culture women always make one wrong stitch in their star quilts, as a reminder that chasing perfection is a futile and impossible process.

I am dedicating this book to a kinder gentler world.

What do you want to learn from this book?

TODAY 2019 WESTERN SOUTH DAKOTA, SOMETIMES REFERRED TO AS INDIAN COUNTRY

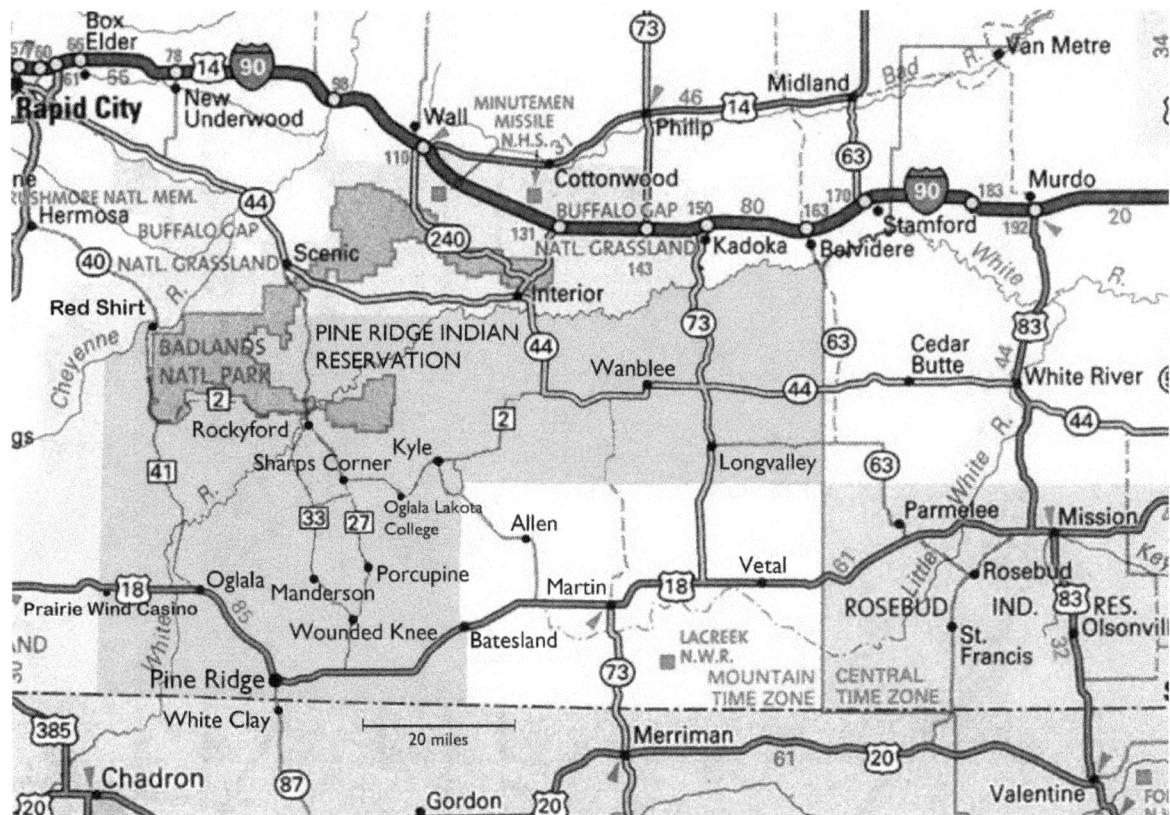

TODAY 2019: I lived in Kyle and Martin. When I lived in Martin from 2006-2008 I commuted, sometimes at night, to Kyle, Wanblee, a desolate drive at night in winter, Pine Ridge, Allen, and Manderson to teach. I often drove on weekends to Rapid City through Scenic, a beautiful open area. I also lived in Rapid City and taught in Martin, 2 blocks from my 2 room modest motel apartment.

AROUND 1850

SIOUX TREATY LANDS AND SURROUNDING AREA
As defined in the 1851 Fort Laramie Treaty as found by the Indian Claims Commission.

1851 Treaty of Fort Laramie Homelands

1851 after Fort Laramie treat. Lakota still intact and powerful, defeated US Calvary several times.

CHICAGO

A beautiful Lakefront. 3 million people and 9 million in the entire metropolitan area.

Named the "City with Broad Shoulders" by the famous author Carl Sandberg

All this came from the abundant natural resources of America, taken from the indigenous tribes. They took care of it

US Steel manufacturing plant in southeastern Chicago-a major steel center

The Schultz family immigrated here to the USA in the 1880's. All my male relatives have middle names of Christian or Christie. Mine is Christie. I like that traditional continuity.

Lutheran Cemetery Blue Island Illinois

My great grandmother migrated here from Poznan Poland in 1882, a kind classy woman. I have always thought that Polish people are very kind.

Me on right, and friends, Malcolm far left, Carl middle Chicago 1955

PALOS FOREST PRESERVE RUNNING PATH-BEAUTY SERENE **My connection to nature.**

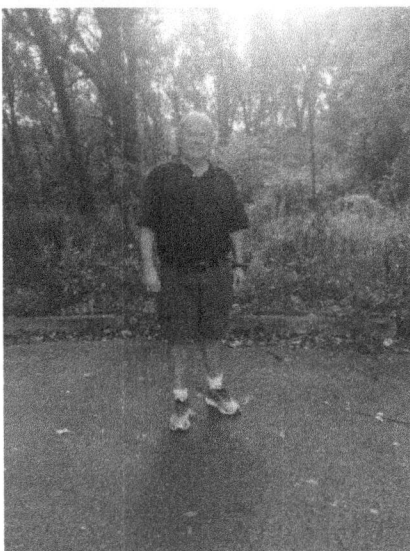

THE ANIMALS

WE ALL LOVE WILD ANIMALS AND OUR PETS

My grandkids great black dog, Burma, who I accompany on numerous walks when I visit. She is very insistent about this twice a day. We have gotten to know each other rather well over 8 years.

BURMA AND ME

SNUGLY MY DOG DACHSHUND CURIOUS LOVING MISCHIVEOUS-SIMILAR TO A WOLF

Painted by Elton Three Starts-Oglala Lakota

WOLF

WOLF SPIRIT-painted by Elton Three Stars-Oglala Lakota

Do you feel the spirit of the wolf looking inside you?

READERS NOTES: What do you know about wolves? And what do you think about them?

BEAUTIFUL ROMAN CATHOLIC CATHERDRAL BUILT 1922

READERS NOTES:

Is there any difference between the magnificent spirit of one of nature's beautiful intelligent social animals and our worship of unseen spirits and saints in a church?

ANIMALS and INDIANS

Buffalo Pine Ridge Indian Reservation

POKER JOE MERRIVAL RANCH

I've had an affinity towards animals on and off my life. And when I was about eight, there were a lot of alley cats in Chicago at that time. We had concrete alleys. They're like tiny little streets. And I came across a black little kitten that was lost it seemed. I took it in and put it in a box. My mother and I fed it milk for a few days. But the mother cat -- and I remember this distinctly -- would be coming around and looking around the bush. And I'd see her out there. So finally after maybe two, three days, my mother said, "The cat has to go." And I said very sadly, "Ok, but I want to keep the kitty". So I took the cat out to the alley and sat her down not too far from her mother. And they went off trotting down this long, concrete alley. I followed them. And they went under a fence into a yard and I called, "Midnight. Midnight." And actually, I'll never forget this, the kitten actually stopped and turned around, the little baby, and looked at me. And I think I could've coaxed the cat back from its mother. It's truly an amazing story. And maybe that shows what a little bit of love does in this world that's so fraught with conflict and intimidation.

I'm going to list various experiences over my lifetime that relate to these topics. Some will make you think. None are made up or exaggerated.

How about <u>African Wildlife</u>? So beautiful, such a landscape, primordial, causes me to feel close to a distant time, a powerful natural force. When I was 22, I was concerned about elephants. My step-father said something insensitive and typical of our society's priorities, "Stop the elephant stuff and get off your butt and get a job!!, very angry he was indeed. How I want to see and experience a herd of elephants. The mass killing/poaching is so horrific. Much is being done to stop this including hired bands of former armed forces combat specialists to hunt down and capture/kill the poachers. But these impoverished natives are not the problem. It's some African game wardens, agents, merchants, Asian brokers, and the superstition healing powers of ivory tusks. What suffering they cause! The same for rhinos, lions, leopards, rare birds and parrots to name a few. And wolves, large fish like cod, tuna, swordfish, sharks. Species numbers are sharply down. Super-large tuna, 5 feet long, are now rare. Coral reefs are fading. Elephants were 1,000,000 (thatz one million) in number in 1975. That dropped to 500,00 by 2005. Now it is down to 350,000 due to more rampant poaching. Any sports hunter who guns down these sensitive majestic animals should be imprisoned and labeled a barbarian.

Amboseli Game Preserve Kenya   Impressive Rare Rhinoceros

I speak about the <u>wolves</u> elsewhere. Pure ignorance and unconscionable cruelty by sports hunters and ranchers. Wolves belong, they are social animals, never attacked a person unless in captivity and teased. My friend had two huge wolfdogs at home and I stood next to them in the kitchen. Just gigantic, shoulders at my hips. I was very nervous and wary. Wolves Belong.

TATONKA-2500 POUNDS

<u>Buffalo,</u> what can I say, hunted to almost extinction by 1900. Only a very small number existed in Yellowstone. My Lakota friend, Dave Chief, said the buffalo are their (Lakota Sioux) brothers. I have films of them at Pine Ridge. Small herds. People don't realize male Buffalo are the size of a small elephant, 2 or 3 tons. I wish I could see the massive herds migrating over the Great Plains. Now that is godlike, natural. In Wisconsin on a small hobby farm near Janesville, Wisconsin a white buffalo was born in 1995, considered sacred. People came there from all over the USA and world, native or not. And me. I was interviewed by local Channel 7 TV about what this meant to me, I said "love". All this was part of an Indian premonition. Two were also born in the Pine Ridge Indian Reservation in South Dakota in a 70 head herd owned by my friend Poker Joe Merrival. I have films of this herd and was driven out among them in a pick-up truck. One day I was standing about 90 feet away and one broke out and came up to me and I actually patted her head. Joe said he had never seen any buffalo do such a thing. And it was the white buffalo!! She had already turned brown as they do by age one. Wow, strange, but in my heart I had tremendous affection and belief about them, all buffalo. You know they are smart and

adapted to our climate unlike dumb cattle that ruin the grassland. In winter they group together and face the wind, unlike cattle that wander apart and freeze. Buffalo also don't eat the grass down to the ground which allows the grass to grow back quickly and healthy, Cattle knaw it right down which causes it to weaken and die. On hills, prior to winter, the buffalo eat the grass on the leeward side of hills, that gets covered with deep snow. The windward side from where the snow comes, has less snow as it is blown away. Here is longer grass, still uneaten, for the buffalo. Smart. Males grow to 2000 to 3000 pounds. Standing stationary, they can jump over a 6-foot fence. And when grazing they stand closer together than cattle, which tend to spread. Of course this is to provide a good defense against predators. Again, smart and instinctual. And their meat is lean and healthy. They can also dig for water with their horns and smell its location. Around Yellowstone park, as they migrate in winter to lower elevations just outside the park, they are harassed, captured cruelly, and sent to slaughter by the State of Montana Wildlife Department. And these are genetically pure, only a small tiny number as such. The remainder of our growing Buffalo herds have some cattle genes. Again, it's the ranchers pushing this slaughter. There is also a hunting season in which hunters kill these majestic American beasts at close range. There is a group encamped up there for the past 20 years, The Buffalo Field Campaign (BFC), that tries to protect the Buffalo, by lobbying the Montana government, educating ranchers, and doing Public Relations around the country. Some have been arrested for trying to block this roundup. Google them. I send them money. And the tourists know nothing about this. They just love to watch the buffalo in summer. But they must help and be made aware. These are real American heroes and patriots, trying to save life. Any school that has the Buffalo as their mascot should teach about this magnificent animal to their fans and students and do something to help them (and wolves). Hear that University of Colorado and University of New Mexico? To use these abused animals as a mascot or summertime relaxation and do nothing about it to learn and help is pure exploitation of them, no doubt about it. What else is new in America sometimes. This great country should know better. Watching Buffalo herds is a spiritual experience. I have Buffalo hide shoes from LL Bean in Maine. They NEVER wear out. Another great place to watch and be near them is Wind Cave National Park near Rapid City, South Dakota. Here they block your car on remote dirt roads. Go, do it! By the way I love Wind Cave Park. Mostly unused by tourists, natural, like it was planned to be by who? God?

I also love Prairie Dogs and their towns. You see them extensively on the Pine Ridge Indian Reservation or national parks but hardly anywhere else because ranchers poison them because they say their cattle walk among them and break their legs on the holes and the grass is eaten away into a brown moonscape. Listen to me. I drove past a prairie dog town on my way home from school (by the way 30 miles over some remote areas) and often stopped to watch them at Pine Ridge. Very soothing, a good feeling. All of them happy. About half a football field in size. And about a quarter mile away in the distance a contented herd of grazing cattle. They lived together in harmony. No cattle in the prairie dog's towns but mostly scattered grass. The prairie dogs' tunnels aerate the prairie soil, strengthening the grass, renewing it for future good growth. And the tunnels are homes for snakes, which eat prairie dogs. After using up the grass the prairie dogs move nearby and repeat the process while the eaten grass regenerates. All in natural balance. And the prairie dogs are also food for eagles and hawks. Poisoning prairie dogs is a cruel agonizing death. And not necessary. It is the ranchers again sanitizing the natural world to exploit it to make money. There is also an immense prairie dog town along the Badlands a mile long! Undisturbed. Our Native Indians still have values that respect nature. Except some corrupted tribal leaders that sell hunting licenses to white men from far away cities for a day of fun sport. Shooting or blasting many of them into a blood mist at a fairly close range. The most bloody kills wins. And they leave the mashed bodies there. I met some of these ignorant killer sportsmen in 2002 in the motel parking lot at the Cheyenne River Reservation in western South Dakota. They had a big beer cooler and were getting ready for an exciting day of executions. I was very angry but held it in. What kind of ignorant human beings do this awful thing? And they probably attended Sunday church services with their families. And many tribal Indian officials approve this-they have lost their native values. So people, when you look fondly at prairie dogs in national parks, these few fortunate ones have escaped from a mass holocaust still going on maybe 50 miles away, remember this.

I had a good friend, a respected elder Lakota, Guy White Thunder, who was Director of Natural Resources for the Pine Ridge Reservation-one-half the size of Connecticut, he stopped aerial hunting of coyotes. He understood natural values.

The Deer. One late afternoon I was diving on my favorite lonely dirt road at Wind Cave Park and I saw a herd of deer 100 meters ahead not far from the side of the road, about 20 of them. So I pulled over, got out of the car, and very stealthily walked slowly forward half crouched down in 3 foot high prairie grass, thinking very loving thoughts about them, they had nothing to fear from me. Closer and closer I came, wow getting so close. Then the solo big buck male rose up on alert and trotted away with about 12 females up a long gradual uphill road to the top. And forward I crept, right into the remaining 6 deer! They looked at me and went back to grazing. I was 3 to 10 feet away from them. I could have reached out and touched the deer next to me. And a light breeze blew their wonderful rawhide scent over me. I was transfixed, awestruck, felt honored. The buck on the hill was braying and clicking for them to leave and join the herd. So I just said, go on deer friends, go join your friends. And they just casually trotted up the hill to rejoin their herd. This was a spiritual connection. Too bad most of you will never experience this, you are so immersed in the American daily culture of distractions and hectic commerce and schedules. My experience was priceless.

The Snake and the Native American temporary academic department chair. When I arrived at the Navajo Reservation in August 2008 I was greeted by my new supervisor and alarm bells went off immediately. I had strong negative feelings and said this guy actually looks kinda like a snake. He was the most intimidating person I ever met and did me grave injustice. When he entered my classroom while I was teaching I literally froze up. I won't go into that long story. I'm sure he has a very good side I never saw. His father was a WWII Code Talker in the Pacific War theater against the Japanese empire. Bravo. A hero. So, I was walking down a dirt road one day in the nearby forest on the middle dirt track in between the two car ruts. Usually I ran along the edge. Thank goodness I didn't this time for some reason. For some reason I was thinking about him when I heard what I thought was the sound of locusts. It was about 2 hours before sunset in August. Shadows were starting to get long. That's funny we don't have locusts here I thought. The pine trees were 100 feet high with scattered grass on the ground. It was shady. I took a few more steps and stopped. The sound continued. So, I looked out at the edge of my line of sight and worked my head back towards me to get a clear view towards my feet to cover the ground for locusts or what was making that sound. And as my head stopped right in front of me, 3 feet away on the edge of the road I saw a vibrating small white tube. Focusing closer was a large rattlesnake, tightly coiled ready to strike me if I moved one inch closer. Perfectly camouflaged, green and brown. A beautiful lethal animal in his domain, waiting for supper to come near (not me, but a rodent). I froze for a moment and looked about and leaped and scampered 20 feet away to the other side of the road. The rattling stopped. I crouched to the ground and stared at him as he remained coiled and turned his head towards me again focused like a laser beam. He did not look friendly. I was amazed to be so close to this magnificent product of our natural world. Then I scampered 30 feet back to where I had started and again crouched down, both of us staring at each other, eye to eye, 20 feet away. He was perfectly still and intently focused at me. I thought about rolling a rock at him but said no, that is wrong, a hostile act interfering with his natural rights, but something most ignorant and frightened Americans would do, some would even be barbarians and kill this magnificent fellow. That's also because our society believes in dominance and the incorrect doctrine that mankind has dominion over the earth. That is stated on page 1 of the Book of Genesis in the Holy Bible. A big reason we have so many problems today and disrespect nature and are overly competitive, super materialistic people. What the Bible means is we have a connection and RESPONSIBILITY to the earth to be good shepherds, to PROTECT it. To live in balance with it. See the difference? Remember folks, the earth and its creatures do not need us humans, they live perfectly well without us, very happily. It seems as though we are the needy ones, actually, parasites to the world

Western Diamondback Rattler

So I left the snake. This is one of the most awesome experiences of my life. I feel honored to have encountered this big ol' boy. I asked the Indians and they said my spirit projected the image in my mind of the tough snakelike supervisor, to create a meeting to resolve this in myself, that I could survive this ego crushing person, and also perhaps achieve some type of mutual respect and reconciliation. I still wonder about this. What a coincidence. And I seldom thought of him. As the famous actor Mel Gibson says in the terrific movie Signs, "there are no coincidences" when referring to the extra-terrestrial invaders. What do you think about the snake? Only Indians would think this way.

Turtle on the Road. Summer of 1996 and my blood was really flowing about animal injustice. We lived next to a small marsh where an old huge snapping turtle lived that I had gotten to know. A short way away was a highway road heading into town with lots of traffic going 40-50 mph. I was going down it and there was the giant turtle ambling across the middle of the highway heading towards the lake on the other side of the highway. This was his families' ancient migratory daily trek. I slammed on the brakes, came to a halt 20 feet in front of him and ran out to look him over. I had to rescue him! I looked up and about 10 cars were backed up including a giant semi-trailer rig. I defiantly raised my arm and outstretched my hand halt. Not a peep, horn, or movement among the traffic. The look on my face must have frozen them. I got a big towel out of the trunk of my car and very carefully wrapped it around the turtle and took him to safety across the road near the lake. Whew! I saved him, what a relief. The traffic still hadn't budged, dead silent. I got in my car and drove slowly into town. One of my proudest moments. I saved this beautiful animal's life who I considered my friend. I set an example to the other drivers about commitment and courage and being an animal caretaker. I could have crushed him or swerved, and another car would have killed him and all would have kept on going. Most of you would have done that you must admit. My god, you couldn't stop traffic for a lowly animal. If I had done that I would still be feeling extreme guilt and remorse, Instead I am happy. A month later the same thing happened on a remote road with no traffic. I ushered the turtle across the road. And I also saved a squirrel, stopped traffic on a busy Saturday afternoon in Grayslake, Illinois on Route 45. Nothing like that has happened again except trying to save some dogs on the Pine Ridge Indian Reservation. More on that later.

<u>Farm Animals-Factory Farms.</u> You all know the horror of these corporate extermination kill compounds that used to house farm animals happily growing up outdoors. No Old McDonald had a Farm anymore, I'll tell you that much. Chickens, hogs, squashed indoors together, artificial light, no movement, all scientific. Organic machines. Animals are miserable. I can't even look at them. That's why we have farm raised organic food. And the cattle, are infused with antibiotics to ward off disease due to their being fattened in giant sized cattle feeding pens, in mud and cow waste. Giant mile long fattening prisons, cattle stuffed with corn feed and growth hormones before the slaughter. You can smell the odor almost a mile away. I once stood next to an isolated hog confinement prison. No windows, A large metal building, very quiet, no pig squeals, noises. Hundreds inside being force fed, no room to move, corporate death for money and efficiency. Never to be free but suffer in silence. Go ahead, eat bacon, we are addicted. But do not forget how these animals suffer. Do not. This is corporate capitalism at its worst.

READERS NOTES: Cruelty to hogs. Should animals be confined for higher productivity and profits for farmer and corporations?

AN ANIMAL YOU KNOW AND THE LAKOTA

DDT crop pesticide almost eradicated the eagle. The Endangered Species Act saved them.

American Bald Eagle

DESHKA rescued Bald Eagle from Alaska. Injured wing at Pow wow near Chicago

I LOVE EAGLES. So do you. The American symbol of freedom. I have seen them on the Great Plains and northern Minnesota and on the Navajo Indian Reservation at the beginning of Canyon de Chelly near Utah and Tsalie, AZ. They are magnificent. I once saw one soaring down the Canyon with a forest on the deep sides with the rushing river below. He landed on a big branch and there was the female waiting for him at their nest. She must have been unhappy because he took off flying above the river looking for more fish. You know by 1960 Eagles were almost extinct due to chemical crop spraying of DDT, which destroyed their eggs. This been banned by the USA and enforced by the EPA and Justice Department. The chemical also poisoned our food and us. Today it is a serious crime to destroy an eagle or pluck its feathers, are sacred to American Indians. Only Indians are allowed to do this with a permit. You know those large headdresses Indians wear? Those are eagle feathers. And only worn by Plains

Indians, not every tribe. Chief Illiniwek had it wrong. I remember a John Wayne Indian movie directed by John Ford and filmed in the southwest like most at Monument Valley Arizona and Utah. Apaches and Commanches as the enemy. Geronimo and Cochise too you know. Not Sioux. But once John Wayne greeted an Apache Chief wearing a headdress in Arizona with "How Kola, Wash-teh, we will hunt the Buffalo". That means Hello my good friend in Lakota Sioux Plains Indian language. But you see these were Apache that had no eagle feather headdress and did not speak "Sioux" nor hunt buffalo. That was 750 miles away north. Funny but a little sad. I have a picture with an injured crippled eagle next to me chained to a perch, Deshka, from Alaska. One of the most beautiful awesome places is the canyon alongside the Cheyenne River heading west along a narrow road towards Red Scaffold SD on the Cheyenne River Indian Reservation. Eagles soar and coast on the winds and eat river fish. This is far away from the America we know. I love it. But scattered along the river are United States Environmental Protection Agency signs with skull and cross bone symbols warning do not eat the fish. You see the river is poisoned. The Moreau River just north heading from the Black Hills eastward just like the Cheyenne River is also poisoned.

William Randolph Heart

Both flow into the Missouri River which has signs in the state capitol, Pierre, that say do not eat more than one fish a month. You see the Black Hills had the largest gold mine in the world, the Homestake Mine, owned originally by Willian Randolph Hearst, the billionaire from San Francisco and owner of the San Francisco Examiner newspaper. Today it is mined out and being converted into a massive underground scientific United States research laboratory. But the Black Hills are porous rock and mines use many toxic chemicals like mercury. These chemicals are leached through the Hills into the water table which flows into the rivers. It is dangerous.

Cheyenne River Canyon-many eagles live here in western South Dakota on Reservation

The Cheyenne River originates just west of the Black hills and flows eastward through the northern edge of the Badlands Park and the Pine Ridge Indian Reservation. But here it is poisoned too. But so beautiful and wild. And guess what?   There is a high incidence of cancer here it seems in the area of Red Shirt Table, a small community in a desolate beautiful area, home of the Bull Bear Clan. The White River also flows 10 miles south of here through the northern end of the Reservation. Guess what. It also originates just southwest of the Black Hills in an area that was heavily mined for uranium from 1945-1985. These mines are deep open holes that leach uranium into the water table and the dug-up ground, called tailings, are blown all over by the winds. I have been all through these areas. The land just west of the Black Hills provided much of the uranium for the US nuclear weapons. There is a trailer camp near there, along the Badlands boundary, and the White River Park Ranger Station. The trailer camp is rustic, here I stayed with my friend Elaine, a few days in the winter. Back in '96 I think. When I first got drawn into all this I just met her by accident somehow. That's how it works out there. Planning isn't really all that necessary, just go. It was winter, mostly cold and sunny. She was staying in her modest RV. Kind of cozy. She had made a little enclosed addition with a wood burning stove where I slept on the floor. She's from western Michigan, out there looking for herself, spirits, helping people. Age 45 then all by herself. That's what happens out there. Attracts people who seem to have some special mission or destiny. Reminds me of Richard Dreyfus in Close Encounters of a 3rd Kind. He was touched by some force (in his case UFO's) and he was compelled to go on his journey. Didn't know why, what for, he just knew he had to go somewhere and he found it. Same thing happened to me, Elaine, others, the compulsion, that came from somewhere. Just starts on ya and builds. Takes you over. You find the reason out later. That Indian Spirit, or whatever, took me over for several years. I knew that area at Pine Ridge was my eternal home. Didn't give a damn about back home in Chicago, America, or my former life. Just didn't matter anymore. What a journey. Really special. It doesn't just happen to everybody. You can't make it happen. It chooses you. And all those people who go to the Rez's each summer to help out and do spiritual ceremonies and learn the Indian Way. Well, most are not really touched. They get a lot out of it, have a great experience, but that's different. I did things there, had experiences that I never will again. I drove all over, picked up hitchhikers, walked into people's homes where I felt pulled. I inspired a lot of those Lakota people. Poor in money but rich in spirit. I'll have more about this to say, and probably in another book.

There's a little homespun café there, run by a Lakota woman. Only serves a few items but it's good. Only place to eat for 20 miles. You see there's a group of 20 RV's and trailers there, almost all workmen from the US Department of Interior or Energy. They are still cleaning up unexploded ordinance from WWII left by all our bombers practicing for Europe and Japan. They say more practice real bombs were dropped there than all of Europe. It's called the Gunnery Range, about 100 miles long and maybe 10 miles wide along the northern edge of the Reservation. Yep they are still picking up bombs and exploded pieces. They also leaked a lot of bad chemicals into the earth out there. These guys live out there and slowly look for debris. And they eat steaks in the Café at night. Big juicy thick ones, you bet. At the start of the War in 1942, the Lakota families that lived there were given two days' notice to evacuate and a few dollars. Typical. Uranium, bombs, chemicals, quite a place to call home. It's also home to some UFO's and ET's they say. I saw some strange stuff out there. Somethings going on I tell you. My Lakota friend said, we don't bother them, they don't bother us. Hmmm…. Wonder if the USA intelligence services were here, well you know, here comes the Army to save the country from Alien Invaders. Blow 'em up!!

There's been cow laser mutilations and crop circles pop up overnight. And BIGFOOT!! He or them are here. Lots of people believe. Amazing. So a friend of mine told me a story his father was going fishing alone up by the White River along the Badlands, only had his dog. So, it's night and he's resting and he feels something odd and there's this bad smell, and rustling in some bushes and small trees. The dog takes off running at it and howls and barks the mystery being disappears .The dog comes back wobbly, nervous, unhurt, but upset. So he heads for home a 50 mile ride. Two hours later when at home the dog drops over dead. I know others who believe it, from Medicine Men to young mothers and students. One 35-year-old woman student said they are spirits, so they come and go and can easily vanish. There was a police daytime incident there. The police were chasing something that just vanished. People rumored about Bigfoot.

One cold sunny morning I took a walk or hike into the Badlands across the road into the unknown. Snow on the ground, saw some coyote tracks, so I let out some really big howls. And from the distance not far away came a bunch of howls back. Oh, that was thrilling. Here I was all alone, communicating with a pack of coyotes. Now I wouldn't trade that for a dinner at a fine restaurant. And another thing, it's really really quiet out there. No human noise. We don't know what quiet is. Maybe just the rustle of the wind, or some crickets in summer. You can hear the blood in your head. I think it would drive some people crazy. See the movie Thunderheart and you will see what this looks like when they race from the tribal police and finish at the Stronghold. That's where the last Lakota hid and lived at the end of their freedom period after 1890 and practiced the Ghost Dance, a prayer to the ancestors to remove the white man and bring back the destroyed buffalo herds. They went to the Stronghold to avoid the Reservation, an outdoor prison.

Oh, and off in the distance, west to the horizon, you can see the outline of the Black Hills. The sacred Black Hills to some people. To me they are a special place. A gentle beauty, unlike the mountains here in New Mexico. The beautiful rolling ground of green and brown. There's some poetry to it, separate from the tourist attraction mess. You know what the traditional Lakota call Mount Rushmore? The Four Faces. Just the right amount of disrespect. I get a kick out of that, I do. You know the Lakota (Sioux) have never collected their court awarded Black Hills money from 1974. It's sitting in escrow, about $1.3 BILLION or more. That is about $ 20,000 per all the Sioux Tribal members. They just can't sell their Hills, cause it's them, their spirit. I'm impressed. Never would happen in America. Oh, did I tell you? The Rez is not America, no way. But the Hills are not the Rez, but are stolen treaty land they want back. I realized then what this summer American National Park tourist frenzy is about. Not pretty. All of us Americans gotta go get our 10 days' worth of American natural splendor to refresh ourselves and buy some local nice stuff for home or just souvenirs. Sure it helps some locals. Here it's also sad to see Indians doing some dances in feathered native regalia to earn some money. Can't blame them, they need money. So the tourists go home, all refreshed, having purchased (remember we are CONSUMERS first and foremost) their years' fill of natural beauty and animal sightings, campfires, and honoring monuments. All the while few know what has really happened in the past or still now for that matter. The human catastrophes, earth scarred and tainted by mining, animal killings. They purchased what they came for. I call it tourist exploitation syndrome (TES). I once had a Lakota man sing me a traditional song on a Rapid City street for money. Maybe he drank it away or stopped at McDonalds, but it was humbling.

And I know, the monument inspires people and represents outstanding American Presidents and all that fun vacation family stuff. It's all right, but most people just don't know enough about the big picture, the clash of civilizations and the complex harmful results.

THE OTHER ANCIENT SNAKE-About 1998 an Ojibwe (Chippewa) spirit man used to come down to Illinois from northern Wisconsin to tell us stories and conduct ceremonies. I remember one story. A long time ago a tribe found a little cute snake in the wild and took it in to care for it, It grew larger, kids played with it, it came along to ceremonies. Eventually the snake grew larger and larger and wasn't so friendly anymore. It seemed moody and sometimes made people feel nervous. Occasionally small animals began to disappear, and it scared and chased horses and groups of small children around the camp. The snake became mean and heartless, and selfish. So the tribe beat its drums and drove the snake away into the woods and across a big lake. And you know what, one day that snake came back, bigger and fiercer than ever, in the form of an aggressive European society and military. It was very hungry.

The Big Horn Mountains and Shangri-La

This is the most amazing isolated place I ever came across. Few tourists go here but there is a lodge and some stores. It is in north central Wyoming along the Montana border. I was heading east from Yellowstone and Cody, Wyoming looking for adventure and the awesome Native American Medicine Wheel circular stone ceremonial ground, way up high in these mountains. I took the steepest road in the nation on up, #14A, up the extremely steep, 10-degree road, and then up to the Medicine Wheel. A place I had to see. The road going downhill has 3 truck runaway ramps. You drive way up there near

10,000 feet and it is alpine tundra like terrain. An off road takes you on up and then you park your car at a ranger station run by a Wyoming Agency and Native Tribes. Then it is an uphill 1.5 mile walk one-way to the sacred Medicine Wheel, just an amazing place with Indian totem prayer ties and dreamcatchers tied to the circular fence around it. These rocks are arranged in a wheel like formation. Google it to see it. A little above you at the mountain top is a US FAA radar station, a white bubble. The funny thing in 2001 I was at the peak of my Indian period and dressed in a hoody, jeans, rumpled, skin weather-beaten, ruddy, and carrying a bag at my waist with all my Indian prayer stuff. And was I surprised. A ranger came up to me and asked if I would like the few tourists removed so I could conduct a ceremony. They thought I was an Indian spiritual man! I was not trying to fool anyone. So I said no and walked around and by myself did some thinking and praying. I had come a long way, both geographically and metaphysically. There were no trees up there. I looked down into a beautiful valley with few trees and wide open deep green grassy meadows with a few cattle grazing. Natural, no other sign of human interference. To me I was transfixed, it seemed like the mystical Tibetan mountain paradise of Shangri La. I'll never forget this experience. Two years later my girlfriend and I camped at the other eastern side of this 70-mile-wide mountain range in the steep rocky Tongue River Canyon. The Lakota and Crow used to hunt there, now it had a few nice cabin homes sprinkled along the narrow rushing river, more like a wide stream. It was mountain lion country, I knew we were being watched as we camped alone in my tiny camping trailer. Exciting to be within the natural world and not malls and stoplights and office parks. A man there said he had a mountain lion sleeping under his porch. What a surprise.

Richard Grass--Richard is or was a dear friend of mine because he died about 2009 from prostate cancer. He lived up in Rapid City, South Dakota at the Dakota Homes Indian Housing. He was low income, so his modest house was free and all his health and dental care. He was about 5 years older than me. He was tall and dark skinned with a great sense of humor. That was common for most Lakota men. Something I really liked about them, a self-deprecating type of black humor. He was a Marine and is buried in a Veterans Cemetery. Richard is a member of the Standing Rock Sioux Tribe. That Reservation is in central South Dakota next to North Dakota. I drove through it and believe me it is wide open flat prairie, hardly any people except in the small communities. You feel like you are somewhere far far away in many ways, not just geography. All those protests about the XL Pipeline were near here. I wish I could bring Richard back, and his sister Mona. Richard is what I would call a self-styled historian and advocate for Lakota rights. To an extent a bit naive, but bold. And all of them also have spiritual parts to them as part of their Lakota world view. Nothing quite like it in the USA mainstream culture. Richard wrote long rambling letters to the US President Clinton and the Queen of England about colonization and exploitation. We went places together and I spent time sitting at his modest kitchen table talking things over and laughing. The table always had piles of newspapers, cut out articles, stacks of copies of this and that covering it. I enjoyed these times together. His son died of alcohol poisoning and liver destruction at age 30 while I was there. He (the son) said he wanted to move to Chicago and live with Ralph (me). I visited him in the de-tox jail. One time I went to visit him in his hospital room when he was ailing, and the hospital chaplain paid him a visit-Protestant religion-and began a serious discourse that he needed to turn to god and pray to save his soul. Must have scared the hell out of him. Inappropriate, insensitive. And he was recuperating, not dying. Right then it reminded me of how all the Christians tried to convert the Indians and used the fire and brimstone save your soul preaching for so long. There was no hell, guilt, punishment in the Indian religions. But kindness, respect for the power healing of nature, and forgiveness. Christianity was another gift from the white man. I tried to help him, but alcohol took its inevitable toll. I began to understand Christian thinking a few years later when I was a teacher at Oglala Lakota College. A white friend owned a Christian book store and was driving me to school one day when I first arrived and commented about the Lakota religion. Matter of factly he told me how the Indians worshipped nature, spirits, had strange ceremonies, didn't believe in a Christian god, as if that they were unenlightened and inferior. Now I finally see that white man's religion coming out, I thought. I was shocked as he was a teacher at the Indian college. Little did he know that by then I had become one of them. I said nothing.

The Native American religions and ceremonies were banned by Federal Law until President Carter in 1978 signed the American Indian Religious Freedom Act. Since then Indian traditional ceremonies have proliferated and the influence of Christian churches has declined.

Richard's great-grandfather, John Grass, fought against General Custer at the Battle of Little Bighorn (Custer's Last Stand) and was the first Treaty Chief at the Standing Rock Reservation. Richard was very proud of that. I remember in the summer of 2000 I moved out to Rapid City and found a job as a airport van driver. I was told to stay out of the Indian Housing neighborhood Lakota Homes because it was so dangerous. Over the years I and my Dachshunds were there many times and there was no trouble, I was accepted and felt perfectly at home. Probably the only white man visitor in 300 homes. Rosalie Little Thunder lived there, the highly respected Lakota artist and Indian and environmental rights activist. I have her on a DVD talking to me about the earth and their history. In 1995 she WALKED from Rapid City across Wyoming to Yellowstone to protest the harassment and killing of Buffalo outside the

Park and conduct spiritual ceremonies in honor of the Buffalo. That's about 500 miles! I admire that commitment. Her family relatives were massacred in 1872 by the US Cavalry. See her picture at the end of the book.

Here's an interesting story. Steven Segal made a movie, On Sacred Ground, about an oil company in Alaska ruining the environment on Indian land. Action packed. In it was a Lakota, Dave Chief, doing a ceremony. He was a Lakota spiritual man I had me at Pine Ridge. He told me the buffalo were the Lakota's brothers. You know Segal is part Indian. I would like the beautifully decorated rawhide jacket he wore. In the movie there was an ugly car, orange and white, a gigantic Chevy Silverado van. I was dropping by Richard's home one day and there was the car! And Davey Chief was inside with Richard. He was given that funny looking car by Segal! Small world it is.

I had two mischievous loving Dachshunds that were my soul brothers. They went everywhere with me, so my Lakota friends named me Two Dogs. The name stuck and that became my common name. I like that about the Indian people. Every time I saw Richard or phoned him the first comments out of his mouth were "How are the pooches?" I thought that was so thoughtful and kind. When my doggie

Starstream died I took him to Richards' and he did a Lakota prayer over him, so wonderful, meaningful. I bawled when he died.

His last day my dog revived and he and his brother and I had a pleasant afternoon, at a church park and a nice drive in the Black Hills. They got out of the car and were sniffing around. That evening he died in my arms. I kept him in the motel with me for 3 days, he lay in my bed while I and his brother slept. He stayed in good shape. I couldn't part with him, so I rented a meat locker and froze him. We visited him a few times. After 3 months I had him cremated. I have those ashes. Precious.

When Snugly died a few years later in my arms I also left him on the living room floor for a few days. It was a very natural thing to do. The heck with conventional thinking. I will never have another dog. I also have his ashes. I consider it a great honor to have been their pal and caretaker. They helped me. I miss them. It hurts.

I went up to the sacred site, Bear Butte, a few times, just north of Sturgis SD. Standing by itself in the middle of the prairie landscape is a monolith, a gigantic bulk of rock maybe 1/2-mile long, and several hundred feet high. A path winds up to the top that takes about 45 minutes to get to the top. In the southern distance is the town of Sturgis and the Black Hills. This place has a real primordial look and feel about it, you almost expect dinosaurs to appear around it. It is a sacred ceremonial place to both the Cheyenne and Lakota tribes. At the bottom are sweat lodges and a State of South Dakota museum and park ranger station. A buffalo herd grazes around it. In the Fall of 2000 on a late Sunday afternoon I hiked up to the top alone. All along the way were Lakota prayer ties on the trees and at the top a sitting area with small rocks arranged in spiritual formations. I spent time here thinking. Few white people travel up here. Unfortunately, nearby in the town of Sturgis the annual famous giant motorcycle biker gathering is held each summer. It is a rowdy sensual noisy at times chaotic four-day party of raucous bikers from all over the USA and from all walks of life. People clad in leather, some women skimpily clad, doing heavy drinking and eating. Cruising slowly on their chrome laden giant-sized bikes showing off and eyeing other people's bikes. At night the parties break out and several new party structures have been built closer and closer to Bear Butte. It goes all day and night. This has upset the Indians and disrupted their sacred site. That political conflict continues with protests, marches, and legal issues. But it is an awesome place-you must see it. The tribes still hold summertime gatherings there with speeches, ceremonies, talks, feasts, and extended families of all ages. I went to one and brought a carload of watermelons for desert, for well over 100 people. The time I went to the top of Bear Butte a thought came to me that mankind has destroyed the earth and not fulfilled the responsibility to be a good shepherd. One must accept the earth will never be quite the same again, but further destruction can be stopped, and the planet made healthy again.

Bear Butte SD Sacred

THE RESERVATIONS—When you enter a large remote Reservation you are immediately in a different place, quieter, back in time, less of taken for granted amenities of life. You can feel it. And when you cross the Missouri River in central South Dakota heading west the land transformation is just incredible. East is flat midwestern farmland and structures. West is wide open rolling hills of brown and green, buttes, and cattle. Little visible infrastructure. The change is immediate. How could Mother Nature have accomplished this sudden transition. The feeling you get is now you again are back in time, the wild west, Indian Country. For sure. Any moment a large buffalo herd will come rumbling over the hilly horizon it seems. Try it. I always loved it. And in central SD the Missouri River is a mile wide. From the east you drive down a long long hill way down to the river. Now at the rest stops are warnings about poisonous rattlesnakes.

Nothing in Indian Country starts on time. They say it starts when it's ready to start. I know all you non-Indian readers like to have everything just so, in order, makes you comfortable. You need a beautiful timeline, logical. Unlike traditional Indian culture.

Long delays can be annoying though. I always started my college classes 5 minutes behind, so latecomers wouldn't miss part of the lecture. Never made any difference. And if students turned in assignments late, that'z ok. Better they complete it when they can then do nothing and learn nothing. They don't collude and don't cheat. Just check me out on Google, Ralph Schultz CNM. You'll see my student ratings.

A few things about Pine Ridge and a few other Indian Reservations. It is quiet. In downtown Pine Ridge Village there is the only stop light on the entire Reservation (1/2 the size of Connecticut). There are no horns blaring, screeching, rumbling, people yelling. For the most part, except for the now commonplace domestic violence arguments people are politely waiting their turn to talk and not be combative like on American TV News shows. Interrupting, pushing, vying to make another point. And their voices tend to be calmer less intense. I always said the Lakota talk like the smooth prairie wind their ancestors lived in. I remember the first time in 1996 I was there for 8 days, and Darin Merrival said to me in that sing song Lakota English accent, "Ralph, you've changed so much since you were here" I quieted down, relaxed, urgency and intensity diminished. Listened. In synch.

The education system tries but the population has too much poverty, social issues, and illness to succeed. So the results are bad. But there are students who go on to distinguished universities nationally known and do well. However, the high school dropout rate is 60% to 70% at Pine Ridge (PR) and other Great Plains Rez's. The 20% who leave the Rez to attend college often return home. They feel lost, don't fit in, and miss their culture and families.

Or the academic pace and rigor is just too intense. Or they are short money. That's why the Indian colleges on the Rez's are sooo important. Oglala Lakota College does a great job educating students and they stay home and get a Bachelor's Degree. And raise families. I taught there 3 years. Most of the students are women, about all are in the poverty zone or close, many work, raise young children, and attend school. And guess what, some drive 10-30 miles on lonely roads, in tough weather. I was impressed. And they work hard in school.

Oh, and the cars are not always in great condition. Some men resent their wives' ambition and try to block them from attending. I usually had 70%-90% women students for business courses. Often the grandmas watch the children when the moms work and attend school. More about Pine Ridge later (and similar Rez.'s).

Financially the reservations have been mostly a cash economy. Very few have checking accounts. Government checks come in and are cashed at the Post Office or turned into money orders to pays bills. No Banks. Most of the population is on government benefits because they are poor financially. They get about the same benefit as someone off the Reservation. Except for the Indian Health Service. All Native Americans who have the minimum blood quotient get free health care but only at Indian Health Service hospitals and facilities. But they are way underfunded, so the care is spotty, inadequate, too remote. Congress underfunds it and complains. Healthcare is the only Treaty Right remaining. These people gave up their land and entrusted their lives to us-the white society-to provide health care, to take care of them. And we failed. There are some nice facilities. I was treated by both an Indian woman doctor and a white doctor who was a federal employee that moved around to VA Hospitals too. He was leaving for Alaska. Care was good. At Pine Ridge there are only about 6 doctors and 20 Nurses to serve 40,000 people, and almost no dentists. Many Indian people have bad teeth. To get treatment it is not unusual to wait a long time and get treated by a tired doctor with inadequate supplies and equipment. Doctors are new MD's working off their student federal loans, older doctors going to the Rez for a year or two to "do good" and career federal doctors. Pay is adequate $125-$175K per year. There is a small housing development for medical personnel that looks like a modest city suburb of town homes nearby, isolated from the Rez town, and looks out of place. Neat, clean, streets and manicured lawns. Like a military base. When a doctor leaves they are given a big ceremonial party and send off with gratitude. And there is a long drive to the medical facility, like 10-60 miles each way for the tribe that does not live in Pine Ridge Village, 5000 people. There is one large clinic about 40 miles away in Kyle, SD. The other 35,000 are spread around this massive reservation. If sick, you need a car that works, gas money, time. And there are only a few dialysis clinics for a population that has high kidney disease.

And these far away isolated tribes are sick with disease. Needs are extremely high. Alcoholism is rampant, and most families have members who are alcoholics. Maybe 30-50% of tribal adults have major drinking problems or might be in remission. Probably all of my 40-60 year old friends at Pine Ridge are recovering alcoholics (now sober). 50% have diabetes and many have heart or kidney disease. I have some friends who had a foot or leg amputated due to diabetes. 25% of children are born with FAS or fetal alcohol syndrome which is why so many students have learning issues. Incidence of cancer is high. Cervical cancer is 500% above the US average rate. 60 % of the homes on the Rez are substandard and overcrowded with 8-15 people living in a small 2-3-bedroom HUD home. Perhaps 25% of the homes have black mold growing inside the walls. There is a multi-year waiting list for public housing. That is why many people live in tents, cars, shacks, old trailers, and dilapidated mobile homes. I have a friend Carol, a hard-working school employee, who had 7 children of various ages, not all her own, in a 2 bedroom home. I have had dinner there. It is clean.

The tribe lives in either small one-story HUD homes in clusters built close together, or in mobile homes, scattered all over the land in various communities.

The average tribal age is 23, the USA is 36. Men's life span is 55, and women about 67. The USA is 78-81 years. There are a tremendous number of young people (90% live below the federal poverty line of $12,000). 40% of the tribal population is under 18. The median income is $4,000 per year. Yes, $335/month. Without federal benefits these people could not exist. I taught in Allan sometimes, a village of 402, with the lowest income in the US. There was a mountain lion that used to roam behind the local general store and gas station. The teacher turnover rate is 8 times the national average. Young teachers come here for 3 years to work off student loans, and other do-gooders arrive and find out reality is too tough. Some are renegade teachers who just couldn't find work elsewhere. Sometimes inexperienced principals do harmful things. At one underperforming middle school a new Lakota principal fired every teacher, 25, even the good ones. Then by August couldn't find enough replacements and had to take back the teachers and request/plead with them to return, but many had other positions.

There's also a lot of favoritism. Often teachers or administrators are fired for some unusual reason with no legal recourse, but show up later at other districts, their alleged transgressions ignored. It's also not uncommon to be set up to fail if you cross someone.

Remember there is no well-developed civil law or courts here. No way to sue someone and even harder to collect a settlement. Pine Ridge has tried to institute a Uniform Civil Commercial Code to legally regulate business transactions and disputes. You can't repossess collateral if you can't find it or enforce a weak court order. The Lakota Fund is a small business lending group financed by east coast big money. By making small loans it has encouraged employment and business on the Rez. Once 12 years ago a large loan ($350,000) to a construction company failed and the Fund seized the collateral and resold it to pay off the loan. Rather than maximize the resale price, the equipment was sold to friends and family at low prices.

It's part of the culture to help others. I had a friend out there living in a small FEMA trailer. A do-gooder from Ohio offered to pay a local contractor to build a small additional outside meeting room for him at a cost of $35,000. The money was sent and, construction began, but stopped with about 1/3 completed. When I was there Vincent showed me a letter he had received from this very upset woman how to get her money back from the builder who was long gone, with all the money. She was going to sue him in the local civil court and see that justice was done and her legal rights enforced. Sorry. But there are no civil courts, no way to do this and no way to find him on this complex and sprawling Indian land. And no one would help her. And there are no addresses. Only Post Office Boxes. Directions are given by landmarks, like in the western frontier days." Take the road up the long hill and turn right by the old church, go down past the trees and the gas station and turn right, up a way is a red house with some old abandoned cars. Be careful, there is a mean dog there." See what I mean? Sad, but I was amused by this unfortunate woman's lack of understanding of how it works out there.

There is a lot of crime on these Reservations and few police. Pine Ridge had 38 officers, 8 under budget, but for a place 50% the size of the state of Connecticut! Think about it. Thatz three shifts and office personnel too. Itz hard to find people and only 44 are funded by the US. The serious 7 crimes are handled by the FBI which are off the Reservation and must travel a long way to do investigations. These crimes are murder, kidnapping, armed robbery, rape and are considered under Federal jurisdiction. All other crimes and public safety issues are done by the understaffed tribal police. And realize this. Crimes done off the Reservation have to be reviewed in local nontribal courts. If a tribal member commits a crime they can escape into the Reservation where the local police cannot follow them, they have no jurisdiction. The Rez is a quasi-independent sovereign nation according to the US Supreme Court. If the police chase someone into the Rez, the case will be disallowed. Sometimes a police car could be in hot pursuit of a grocery store robber, and when approaching the border, phone ahead and get permission from the tribal police to enter the Rez to continue the chase. Some tribes have prearranged agreements with local authorities to permit entry. This is also true of civil matters. I once was unknowingly one month behind in a child support payment being paid to Washington State. They sent the tribe a letter requesting permission to garnish my wages. When I found this out, I paid it. But they could have said no, or I could have paid a fee to a tribal official. See, these places are a different country.

I recall many of the windows on the old public housing rental units had broken/cracked windows allowing cold air inside the home in the frigid winter. Windows were covered with taped down plastic. Maintenance was often spotty. People begged me for money (like $200) to buy propane to heat in early winter because the propane allocations were often late or underfunded. Sometimes rather than plead, people developed plausible schemes to coax your money, like a relative far away was dying and they needed gas money. I can't blame them if you are desperate. Sometimes I got angry, but it was necessary and let's just call it socialism, or Robin Hood. I and others had extra money, they didn't, and they had to heat their homes and feed their families. When propane deliveries were late, which could be 3-4 weeks, people turned the heat down to 50 degrees F. inside when it was 10 degrees outside. Now try that. In the winter of 2007 there was a major delay and shortage of propane due to delays getting approval from the Federal Government caused by the Republican Party doing budget cuts.

So to my astonishment <u>Hugo Chavez, President of the socialist Venezuelan government</u> provided $720,00 of free propane to any needy tribal members without the usual red tape delays. What a hero!

Venezuela owns the American oil company CITGO. So before you start criticizing socialism and the "unfree" "un-American" countries, you ought to remember this act of charity. People First. This is just one reason why I tend to favor some socialist type states, with all their flaws.

The average life span for Reservation Indians is very short. I have seen numbers from 50-60 years for men and up to 65 years for women. In the USA those years are 78-83. Shocking. But poverty, isolation, disease, obesity, and lack of money takes its toll. I remember one 16 year old who told me his dinner was microwave popcorn. His parent were out somewhere. Remember, these large expansive remote Reservations are in reality an undeveloped Third World Country. Politically they are too, as small entrenched family elites tend to run them and favor themselves with benefits and jobs. Election results tend to be unclear, and if you complain about anything excessively, or resist policies, you lose benefits and opportunities. You may be sent to the end of the 2-year housing waiting list, or maintenance for your home is lacking. And it always helps if your family is friendly with police and judges. So what else is new?

One day I was standing by the Wounded Knee hill cemetery thinking and the thought came rushing into me, "These are really STRICKEN people" Yes they are. So when you here the unemployment rate is 70% or more it is because most people can't work, they are too ill. Or lack cars to drive 20-100 miles to a job in all types of rough weather. And they lack skills and everyday work habits. It's overwhelming. Tribal and the federal government jobs are sought after for the educated or connected but in short supply. It is almost impossible to pick yourself up by your bootstraps here, since there are no straps. I once saw three 10-year olds sniffing aerosol spray out of empty cans in a trash heap to get high. But for the most part homelessness is not an issue, because someone can always stay with a friend, or relative, lots of uncles, aunties, and cousins. It seems that Indians still are a bit nomadic. Many come and go from the Rez to live with relatives around the Rez and in other cities like Denver, Cheyenne, and Phoenix. They may work for a while and then eventually head back home to their Rez. That's why the US Census Bureau undercounts the Indian population. I knew someone who went to Nebraska for 2 months to pick potatoes.

I remember driving through Lodge Pole, Montana on the Crow Reservation heading to Wyoming. I was shocked by the poverty and the tired decrepit homes and potholed dirt roads. These Reservations all have similar issues. The atmosphere was muted, slow, cautious.

I spent some time on the Crow Rez. I walked and drove the entire Custer battlefield. The Lakota have a separate place there which honors their lost fighters and not the US Cavalry.

I stayed at a motel there and met a white man living there who related to me some stories. Often scholars, professors, anthropologists (Indiana Jones?), came from universities out east to study the battle and stayed for a while at this little motel. And on two occasions in the middle of the night the bed started shaking, room rumbling, whistles screeching, and a roar from the walls. Well, both times the professors were gone the next morning. I had somehow met Joe Bear Cloud on the radio and telephone a few years before in 1999. He was both an artist and a spirit man. He sent me Christian songs sung in Crow by his native choir. Beautiful. I went out there twice to meet him and interviewed him on tape. We became close friends. Of all things he sent me a huge thick bearskin fur rug which I still have 25 years later. He invited me out to the massive Crow Fair annual August event that has 10,000 Crow members and has a 1,500 teepee village. It attracts 40,000 visitors. Joe once took me on a ride through the center of the reservation to Yellowtail Dam and a sacred burial ground of Pretty Boy, a famous respected chief. No white people ever go there. It was quite an honor. We each went off by ourselves to pray. Joe saw an eagle. When I went over to stand by the grave Joe said a large Crow circled overhead, something he had never seen before. I feel honored to have been there. On the way back, we stopped at a stone medicine wheel on the ground, on a ranch, left there for 250 years. Joe said, "you are different, you have a nice soft way about you". My Indian spirits were taking me over. I was being transformed. Indeed.

The land south of the Pine Ridge Indian Rez just over the Nebraska border is the Sandhills and extends south for over 100 miles. Look at a map. I drove it to the Platte River. It is desolate. Rolling hills of sand covered by grass and low cactus here and there in sunlit areas. Nothing, no human signs except a town of 10 old structures, a lonely tired store and gas pump, maybe a post office. No cell service. Long rolling large hills. Fascinating, awesome, a little scary, you are alone out there. There is a park outside Chadron Nebraska with feral donkeys. I had stopped the car and looked up and staring at me was a donkey two feet away, eye to eye. We stared and "talked". Never forgot it. Felt good.

I lived in Martin SD almost 3 years, 1001 people, 50% Lakota. Stayed in a very modest motel apartment. Played golf and ran on a very hilly golf course when I was 60, still in shape. Drove just outside of town to see to see antelope and look for the elusive cougar in the buttes. I saw cougar tracks in the snow on the golf course. It was also seen at 5 AM at a street intersection. Rattlesnakes used to come into town during dry hot weather and lay on watered areas like lawns and the high school football field. One day I looked at the outdoor temperature-114 degrees, you got it. I sat in it for the experience for 15 minutes.

Saturdays are Prime Rib nights at the country club modest buffet, at a modest private golf course open to the public. That was my weekly fancy dinner. Martin was the scene of some very serious civil rights marches in the past led by people like Russell Means. Life is different there. Strangely, my former girlfriend's ex-husband is from there. Such a small obscure town. What a coincidence! And she was mostly from Italy and Spain and Washington DC. I always thought this was some special sign we had a permanent connection. She lives in Los Angeles now, and is a major supporter of animal rights abuse issues.

I have to tell you about two characters from Martin. I really liked them both, wonder about them. Yogi, about 55, was a great guy, sober, a recovering alcoholic with diabetes. He walked each day for health. He told me stories about the Lakota and the City of Martin history. He is authorized to conduct sacred Lakota sweat lodge ceremonies. A very humble man, married, family, who really tries. He lives in an incredibly unusual almost makeshift modest home needing repairs but clean and proud. He actually bought it, paid too much. What else is new, picked off by the white man. Maybe $35,000. Very crowded, one bed is moved into the kitchen each night. For a parting present he gave me a large rock he found on his property. And a carving of a frog he made. Then there is Elton Three Stars, a beautiful name, a well-known Lakota artist. He has some paintings in Paris and the local college center. I gave him $400, a small fortune for him, to paint three incredible pictures of a wolf, and my two dogs, Snugly and Starstream. They are incredible because they have a texture to them and appear lifelike. He captured their spiritual essence. I have them with me. They are my most prized possession. He did his painting in the morning after a joint to calm down his shaking hands from alcoholism. He was tall and lean, like the natural Lakota frame, before bad food caused obesity. The Lakota have flat lean backsides (the place you sit down on), and in fun call the white people "bubble butts" with their rounded rear ends.

He had bad teeth, no dental work. Said a swig of vodka in the morning took care of them. He was a dumpster diver. One time I bought a watermelon for him and the bros at the park but forgot a knife. He went over to the park trash dumpster and pulled out a long shard of sharp glass and began slicing the melon. I said goodbye, none for me. He knew the police because of a little petty crime, drunkenness, maybe a candy bar he walked off with. One time the police cruised by and he thought they were after him, so jumped into a dumpster. After a minute he peeked out with the lid up an inch, you could see his eyes. Funny. He mostly lived in a little one room shack behind the grocery store, kind of like a kid's small cardboard and plywood playhouse. A space about 4 feet by 5 feet and 4 feet high. His hideaway. He did stay with other friends however. He had a place to sleep, some blankets, personal stuff, Lakota spiritual carvings. It was surprisingly clean and neat. I have wondered how he is, probably died of alcoholic liver disease.

Well Indians ain't all nice. One of the cruelest people I ever met was Karen Tall Feather. She poisoned a puppy I loved and froze a big dog she kept chained up. At 11 PM one night I snuck over and put 2 blankets around this sad dog and some food. It was about 15 degrees. I had to leave and the poor old guy whimpered. Next day she said she was going to have me arrested for trespassing and froze him again. A neighbor I knew took the dog and that was the saving grace. A police officer eventually killed him when he growled as the police officer approached him. You see that officer used to scare the dog in his black uniform when he came over to break up domestic disturbances at her trailer. I also was taking care of a dog who would come stay outside my door by the car next to my front door. I fed him, petted and played with him. The same police officer shot him when the dog was walking behind a food store by the garbage cans. He was a slow kid, and his father was a very powerful Indian politician, so I couldn't do anything. It's been over 10 years and I still feel sad when I think of this. And angry. Indians also do mean things to both Indians and white people. I used to walk my dachshunds around the town. For some reason Indians there liked chihuahuas, Mexican little yappy dogs with sharp little teeth. These dogs multiplied and hung out in packs. One time they attacked us and surrounded us, yipping and lurching inward. I picked my dogs and had a tough time getting away. Must have been 10 of 'em. On Saturday afternoons my dogs and I would take a 50-mile drive to Nebraska through open terrain, sandy and hot. We stopped at a nice tiny town, walked around, and drove back, looking out the window. Became a weekly melancholy ritual.

I worked at <u>Little Wound High School</u> for a few months in Kyle on the Rez. They never said the Pledge of Allegiance. A Lakota man would come on the loud speaker and recite Lakota prayers and sing melodic beautiful songs. I liked that. Sometimes I would talk about Lakota history to the 15-year old students, they knew very little. And ALL the students were on the free Federally funded school breakfast and lunch programs. Often these were the only warm full healthy meals they got. I ate them for $2.00, they were good. Pancakes, bacon, fruit, scrambled eggs, toast, cereal, juice, milk for breakfast and good hearty lunches. And to think the US Congress tries to limit these programs to balance the budget. But our soldiers eat well. The convenience stores are full of fried sugary foods that are killing them. You should see the gas pumps outside, beat up, old, barely working. Except for one station in Pine Ridge Village, Batts, famous and ultramodern with good food and groceries, TV screens. Owned by a white man, like most of the business there. And there ain't many stores. There is only one large grocery store on the Rez and a few small tightly packed ones. And no neon signs. Some signs are handmade, lines crooked, words put on with stencil and spray paint. Like the words "Betty's Kitchen" for a restaurant in a woman's kitchen, only daily specialties served.

There is very little business on the REZ. It is too isolated. But the people are not natural entrepreneurs and business people. If you had a bakery your friends and relatives might stop by and expect free donuts, after all, you're family. They are truly socialists, not capitalists. My white supervisor said the Indians major emphasis is taking care of one another, not really accumulating wealth, although they all need some money. I once took a poll of my economics students. "Do you prefer socialism or capitalism?" 11 students said socialism, 2 capitalism. One Indian lady said she wanted to be taken care of and not worry. One white man married to an Indian said capitalism was just to rough and competitive, harmful. And two others said capitalism, so they could make lots of money. There you go. And these students I had were all hard workers, and pretty smart too. Full of hope for a good future. And there still is the idea that the land is sacred and needs to be protected. The tribal people own very little land. The US Government owns most of it in Trust and white people have a chunk for ranching and farming. These "white people" ranchers do pay land rent, but for years the BIA kept rents very low. When rents were raised in 2007 many white ranchers were very unhappy. If you want to see a different world visit a large isolated Indian Reservation. The entire tribe lives in the same small HUD cluster housing or mobile homes. Those with real good tribal jobs have two modern trailers with nice furniture inside and new SUV's. Indians are good teachers, government bureaucrats, administrators, and artists. I have never seen so many people with natural artistic ability as the people living at Pine Ridge. Most have little training, maybe their grandfather showed them. And art schools? Forget it. It is innate in many. They also have medicine men. Some do wonderous things. Others are showman. But all this emanates from the right side of the brain that is intuitive.

Rapid City has many pawn shops; I never saw so many. It is where Indians go to borrow money by putting up their belongings as collateral. You can get some beautiful Indian jewelry here and Star quilts. It is kind of sad. Indian people tend to have a challenging time getting loans. I remember driving around. Some Indians had gotten to know me as a supporter of their culture and political difficulties. I had long beautiful hair then and sometimes they acknowledged me with the Hey Bro sign. I liked that. I did a lot of good out there.

There's a beautiful store out there, Prairie Edge, that sells the most beautiful art and all kinds of Lakota things. See their on-line catalog. They have a beautiful Buffalo hide for sale that I always wanted. Check it out on Google. I wrote a proposal for an interracial healing meeting which I sent to several sources for funding. The closest I came to getting the funds was from Jane Fonda, the famous movie actress. I always respected here. It never happened. There are almost no Black or Jewish people there. I saw 3 Black people over 10 years. Two were tourists and one worked in the drive through window at Burger King. He also gave me the Bro Sign. As far as I could tell also few people of Jewish descent. Most of South Dakota is ethnically from northern Europe and are fair haired blonds. The Indians comprise about 12% of the population and are in stark contrast with their dark skin and hair. There was no confusion who was who with a few exceptions. I love the Black Hills with their rolling brown and green colors. As you drive out of town gradually you get into what call rounded mountains with easily traversed winding roads. There is a comfort about driving there. Up high are a lake or two. I did some hiking there. On the western side it gets pretty isolated. Some tribes have purchased large parcels of land here. I drove through there and had the road blocked by a herd of Texas Longhorn cattle. Southwest of the Hills there is an area of former uranium mining back in the 1950-80 period. Piles of excavated dirt were left that blew about contaminating the Cheyenne River. To the west is Wyoming, a magnificent state. You can easily see herds of antelope. Go to Devil's Tower, the monolith in Close Encounters of a Third Kind. It is eerie and magnificent. As you come over a hill after a 30-minute drive, there it is in the distance. It is a sacred Lakota and Cheyenne site where ceremonies are performed. I would like to visit it again. It is powerful. Funny thing, the day I drove there the area was full of leather clad bikers going on their summer adventure trip. Culture clash again. When you drive back from The Hills heading into the Rez, the land is flat with some rolling terrain and green 10-inch-high native prairie grass. It reminded me of an ocean of grass. The road heads into the small community of Oglala. One thing that stands out how is tired looking everything is and uniform. It is poverty that grinds on amid a people who make the best of it and maintain their cultural traditions. I almost went to work there in the middle school. I would have lived right there next to the school in modest teacher housing, intermingled with all the tribal community members. Almost all the white teachers drove 35 miles each way to live in the white Black Hills town of Hot Springs. There are outcropping buttes here that have trees growing, a narrow forest that goes on for 20 miles. The towns I like to travel to are Hill City and Hot Springs, a partial tourist city where I stayed sometimes at a motel with a large buffalo sculpture outside. I remember I checked the classical novel Macbeth out of the library and read it for the first time. I drove all over the hills exploring towns and scenery. Hill City below in the Black Hills. I stayed there in a motel with a big buffalo statue.

Badlands east of the Black Hills, northern edge of the Pine Ridge Reservation

PICTURE OF ME 2002 BLACK HILLS LONG HAIR

The Lakota Oyate [People] gave me the name TWO DOGS because my 2 dogs were always with me. That was neat. Typical Indian. Name associated with a characteristic.

Some other people I knew there. I met <u>Floyd Hand</u>, a spiritual historical man and social activist. He was a powerful person. I remember the first time I met him at his nice neat trailer home. He looked at me and said, "You have sadness in you, something happened when you were eight years old" I was amazed. That is the year my birth father disappeared which seriously hurt me deep inside my heart and soul. How do you explain that? He sent me to see Zach Bear Shield, a spirit man near Wounded Knee. I did my first sweat lodge there. The heat was unlike I ever experienced before. I had some realizations as he chanted in Lakota around the red-hot stones in total darkness with some other people. His place was in an area you approached on a rutted bouncing dirt road, not far from the massacre site in 1890. There were lots of massacres in the 1800's mostly done by the US Cavalry, wiping out entire villages. The soldiers were often given small bottles of whiskey to drink before riding in to kill innocent people.

You know the USA has never officially apologized to the Indian Peoples for destroying their homeland. In 1999 Kevin Gover, a Pawnee, and Director of the National Museum of the American Indian, came close when he apologized for the horrible way the Bureau of Indian Affairs had treated Indians and cheated them repeatedly over mining and cattle grazing rents. He was Assistant Secretary of Indian Affairs. But never a President. It should be included in every Presidential Inauguration, a brief prayer of thanksgiving and remorse. European countries are mostly populated by their original ethnic group. It wasn't necessary to destroy an existing native population. If the US had to repurchase the existing American continent, then at today's prices it would be financially impossible. We (USA) got it for free.

<u>Tony Blackfeather and Garfield Grass Rope</u> were the Lakota unofficial representatives to the UNPO or United Nations Peoples Organization in 1992 to 2004. The UNPO is an organization of all the indigenous peoples of the world without their own country. This is American Indian tribes, Aborigines, Kurds, Amazon rain forest people, mountainous Laos, Basque, about 370 million people worldwide. You see in Indian Country some people just start doing or become a leader naturally they say based on effort and accomplishment. So, these two just started going to the yearly meetings in Geneva Switzerland. They did not represent the tribal government but the Lakota people. White people bought them airline tickets and provided a place to stay in Geneva. At Pine Ridge Tony lived in a shack without running water. The walls were covered with newspaper articles from places and events he had been. There were few pieces of furniture and no TV. An old beat up computer was there. I often found him chopping wood

or fixing his old car. People from around the world would call him or occasionally stop by to talk. He died of throat cancer 12 years ago. Tony once told me about 2002 that his contacts in the UNPO group told him the USA was the largest violator of human rights in the world. I was shocked. The Declaration of Human Rights establishing the rights of Indigenous Peoples was approved by the United nations in 2007. The US, Canada, New Zealand and Australia resisted signing but eventually did a few years later. Russia also was slow to approve it and abstained from voting. In 1997 I casually walked into a large meeting in the Black Hills of natural leaders (not elected officials) from several tribes around the country. The Indian Law Alliance from New York City was there. They were preparing a draft of the Working Copy of the Declaration of Indigenous Rights. I have that marked up copy. Just amazing that I could walk in alone. I had been told about the meeting, so I just drove there up in the Black Hills one Saturday morning. There formal invitations aren't necessary, everyone is welcome. You see, out there as one explores the area, and themselves, you tend to go places that just happen, they say, where you are supposed to be. These people are called Natural Leaders. They aren't elected, but just arise and do something significant, start something, and then the people may follow them or not. In the 1800's a person became a natural leader like Crazy Horse, Sitting Bull, Red Cloud, or Geronimo. By the way, I am shocked the US Intelligence Services called Osama Bin-Laden "Geronimo" as his code name. Geronimo was a freedom fighter, a medicine man, and a natural leader for his people, the Apache Tribe in Arizona in 1880. It's in the movie Zero-Dark-Thirty. His brave deeds and wise decisions caused the people to admire him and believe his leadership. The US Cavalry killed his people and stole their land and subjugated their civilization. Another example of US ignorance, disrespect, and arrogance. So, if a leader began to decline, make mistakes, another natural leader who would arise from the tribe. To make major decisions the tribal or clan council, the elders, would meet. They needed a 100% consensus to approve an idea. One person could hold out and stop it. But they talked and talked, smoked sacred pipe, until they came to an agreement. There is also Natural Law which are non-codified rules on how to live a good life This leads to Restorative Justice. A person who commits a crime may go to a tribal jail or informal prison, but the objective is to reform them, teach them how to live, how to heal, and get back into the tribe as a positive influence. It is not for punishment. This idea is slowly seeping into prisons with local Indian authorities for minimum security prisons. Most tribes have what is called progressives or full bloods that are in opposition to tribal elected governments that work closely with US agencies. They are trying to bring back old ways and consider the tribal governments agents of the colonial USA and illegitimate. These people are also called full bloods because most have high percentages of pure Indian blood and darker skinned. Some are lighter skinned or whites that share these beliefs. The tribal official leaders and their extended families tend to be lighter skinned with more white blood and dominate the Rez. In the early Rez days the full bloods were persecuted and lived further out from the main Indian towns that had the tribal government and Bureau of Indian Affairs. The Indians there integrated with whites and became powerful, often times corrupt. The full bloods still tend to be discriminated to this day and live further away from the larger tribal centers. This is what happened on the Pine Ridge Reservation in the 1970's. They say the Iyeska or mixed breeds ignore many Indian traditions and don't know if they are Indian or White. It gets complicated. And someone has to deal with US government agencies and complex regulations and planning.

Alex White Plume has been a Lakota rights leader. He grew hemp to provide a living for his people but was raided by the State of South Dakota. I had purchased a buffalo which he was going to keep for me in his own herd of 20 animals. His wife Debra is also an activist.

Vincent Blackfeather is a friend of mine and a spiritual man. He has some land outside of Kyle, SD. He has about 30 used cars in his yard that he uses for spare parts for his vehicles and for other people. I have been in "sweat" lodge ceremonies with him. He and his wife live in a FEMA (Federal Emergency Management Agency) used surplus trailer (not fancy). His is also an historian.

Frank Eagle Tail from Cheyenne River Rez and the village of Green Grass was a good friend of mine, like brothers. I took Frank with me on some trips around the Black Hills and covered his expenses. He told me many stories and supported his people. Once we were driving in the Black Hills and came to a stop light. Next to me was a truck with a white person looking down at me and he made fun of me by patting his open hand against his mouth and making the Indian chant. I had long hair and a dream catcher hanging from the mirror. I now know what it was like to be a victim of discrimination (a little bit). It also happened another time in St. Louis, Missouri. I learned something, no fun. Frank died of a massive heart attack 10 years ago. He smoked 2 packs of cigarettes a day. I miss him. By the way for most Lakota men the cigarette of choice was Lucky Strikes or Camels no filter. Tobacco is a major sacred substance out there used for ceremonies. And they like their tobacco strong. He was from Green Grass, a small community on the Cheyenne Rez along the Moreau River. It is the home of Arvol Looking Horse, the Lakota well known spiritual man and Keeper of the Sacred Lakota Pipe. Here the village horses run free and hangout eating grass by the playground. They may walk up to your car to say hello.

Ed High Bear from Cheyenne River was also a great friend of mine. He lived in the modest Lakota Homes development with his wife and a grown child or two and grandchildren. Crowded but clean. He was like a brother to me too. You know once you are good friends with a Lakota you are friends for life no matter how much time has passed since your last meeting. Blood brothers is true. When I visited I was always given a hearty modest meal, coffee, or cake. I always felt a very warm comfortable feeling when I was there, my worries just vanished. I always wondered whether that was some spirit power at work. He and his wife tried to adopt/raise their granddaughter as their daughter was declared incompetent by the State. Lots of paper work and interviews. You know what? That modest house was declared inadequate, too many people there, wall electric plugs not up to current code, etc. So their granddaughter was shipped off to a white couple in Virginia 1500 miles away. They were not allowed to see or talk to her. Heartbreaking. See? The cruelty of the "system".

Many Indian children are raised by their grandparents. A law was passed to prevent Indians kids from being adopted by whites if an Indian person was available and deemed adequate. The Indian Child Welfare Act was supposed to stop this type of thing, but problems still continue. My dentist, a white person, adopted an Indian girl. When she became 16 she ran away to the Reservation to live and be raised there with "her people". This is an on-going dilemma. White people mean well, but many discourage letting their children to know Indian culture. Ed died of bone cancer 10 years ago at age 58. He was in pain.

You have all seen Indian Pow-Wows or get togethers. In the past clans got together who hadn't seen each other all year to celebrate and reconnect. The dancing, drumming, is hypnotic and the food is tasty and plentiful. There also is an honoring ceremony for military veterans which I have been in. Indians people have a large enlistment in the armed forces. It is an escape from the reservation and part of a warrior tradition. Unfortunately, many return to the Rez and friends and family and can't adjust to being away. I always remember what I was told about War. "Honor the warrior, NOT the war". Pretty neat. Makes sense.

The Sun Dance is a summer ritual which tests the limits of human endurance and spiritual commitment. I have watched some as a supporter. It is 4 days. The participants, who are men and women, Indian and non-Indian, dance and chant and blow eagle whistles in a circular area around a cottonwood tree. They are tethered to the tree by a long leather rope. An eagle claw pierces your chest and this leather string is fitted through the two holes pierced in your chest. The people move forward and back, drums are playing, and it is exhausting under the sun in 90-100 degree heat. The group stays together four days and fasts and has little to drink. Each person determines how many days they can endure. Some faint in the sun. During the dance, some people pull backwards in time with the sacred drumming and chanting, and pull the eagle claw out of their chest which leaves a ripped hole in the skin that is healed by herbal remedies. It leaves a scar. After 4 days they have a giant feast. This is a sacred ceremony to honor the creator Wakan (holy) Tanka (large) or Great Spirit. There also is a Vision Quest. Here a person is given a spot on a hill and must sit on a blanket 1- 4 days without food or water. Sometimes water or gator-aid is provided on a limited basis. It does not matter what the weather is like. The original reason for this was to get a vision of what to do or how to lead your life. Crazy Horse, the Lakota warrior who fought General Custer, did get one that gave him his ability to fight. Sitting Bull, the Lakota leader, did a ceremony before The Battle of Little Bighorn (Custer's last Stand) and saw soldiers falling into their large encampment. That is what happened two days later, as the soldiers attacked and were stricken with arrows, falling down to the ground.

The white people often thought the Indians were a little "spooky, mysterious" The Indian reservations were miserable places, in effect prison camps. Food was very unhealthy, a bad diet and supplies, blankets, and clothes were poorly made. Often dishonest Reservation white governors took some of the supplies and resold them for personal profit, leaving the Indians with a food and clothing shortage. People could not leave the Reservation without a permit. Health care and education were bad. (and still are). Some ceremonies were outlawed so the Indians went to the far reaches of the Rez to do them, like the Sun Dance. Children were separated from their families for a year at a time and sent to Indian boarding schools to be "civilized" Speaking their language was forbidden and punished. Their hair was cut short and they wore white man's clothing. The tribe was forced to live in ramshackle cabins. All this broke the spirit of the Indian people. All treaties that were written to protect them were violated. I had a friend, Kathy Yellowhawk, who in the 1960's at age 14 while attending a boarding school was punished by being forced to pray for 2 hours on her knees on a hard floor.

Gerald Ice and Norma Ice (his sister) and family were friends I met by a strange coincidence. I was in Wounded Knee trying to find Zach Bear Shield's place in 1996. I stopped my car and walked up to a mall house to ask for directions. As it turned out this family was active in ceremonies and teaching white people the Lakota way. Even more amazing, the grandmother was the sister of Wallace Black Elk, a well-known spirit-history man who had I listened to on the radio 6 weeks before and read his book. He was an inspiration to me to come out to Pine Ridge. How could this random coincidence have happened I asked myself? Lydia lived in a little log cabin, one room but divided by Indian curtains. It was very nice, cozy, a trip to the past. Norma once told me "We are not Americans, not Native Americans, not Indians, but Lakota People" I never forgot that comment.

You have to see the round Indian made museum at the bottom of the hill at Wounded Knee. The inside is painted with beautiful and powerful pictures, artwork, and historical information. Gary Rowland helped run it. He lived in Wounded Knee. He chopped a lot of firewood for resale. We became friends.

During the Wounded Knee 10- week siege against the FBI in 1973, he was a teenager supply runner. He went out at night down the complex ravines, avoiding FBI and Federal Marshalls surrounding the Hill to get ammunition and medicine, supplies. There are many other people like Dorothy and Joyce Sunbear, a retired teacher. Joyce was raped at the same time by three white men when a teen and still suffered from that experience. There are the Locke sisters, Carol, Sandra, and Marlene from Porcupine. Marlene also lives in a modest little two room cabin with limited utilities. Her parents had lived there.

Russel Means, Dennis Banks and Leonard Peltier. Russel appeared in the media as the Indian Chingachgook in the movie The Last of the Mohicans and on the Larry David Show. He also wrote an excellent book, Where White Men Fear to Tread. These men were well-know Indian leaders and fought for Indian Rights. They were arrested by the FBI and acquitted, except for Leonard Peltier who is serving two life sentences for killing two FBI agents in a shoot-out in 1977 at Oglala at the Pine Ridge Rez. Many believe he was framed. He might have been falsely convicted.

See the movies Incident at Oglala (Robert Redford producer) and Thunderheart (Val Kilmer & Sam Shepard) to understand this complex situation. There is strong evidence that Leonard did not commit this crime, but all appeals were denied. He has not been granted parole numerous times despite the fact his health is failing, and he has been a model prisoner. Presidents Obama and Clinton denied commutation of sentence despite tremendous support from the public including major civil rights leaders (Nelson Mandela, Rev. Desmond Tutu, Rev. Jesse Jackson, Coretta Scott King, Mother Teresa, the Dalai Lama, the European Parliament, Veterans for Peace, and Michael Gorbachov (Soviet Union leader). The FBI applied much pressure not to show compassion to Leonard despite evidence inconsistencies and did a demonstration outside the White House in 2000 to stop Presidential commutation of sentence. He has been in prison 40 years. He has written his ideas about life and prison in his book My Life is a Sundance: Prison Writings published by Harvey Arden, a retired National Geographic writer with a major interest in Indian history. He also written a play about Leonard. Another great detailed history about this issue is In the Spirit of Crazy Horse by Peter Matthiessen. Also read Bury My Heart at Wounded Knee by Dee Brown.

(a famous book about the destruction of American Indians from 1850-1900),

and Lakota Woman by Mary Crow Dog. I have read all of these and about 30 more including the actual Lakota-USA Treaties of 1851 and 1868 word for word. Of course, they were quickly violated.

In the 1970's Pine Ridge had the most murders per capita in the USA. There was a civil war going on between the official tribal leadership and the traditional full blood people. AIM had been invited to help the full blood people who were protesting civil right violations and poor leadership, rigged elections. In 1973 was the Wounded Knee 71-day US/Tribal/Government vs. Traditional Peoples stand off or siege. It was an international media event. During this time GOONS, or Guardians of the Oglala Nation set up roadblocks, searched people for weapons, and even drove through isolated Wanbli, randomly shooting up the town. Several people were hurt or killed in their homes by bullets. This intimidation continued which brought in more AIM (American Indian Movement) outsiders to help the People (OYATE). Oyate is the Lakota word for the nation, the cohesiveness and value system, tradition. Literally it means the people. The GOONS were a private paramilitary group of tribal volunteers working closely with the tribal police, Federal Marshalls, and the FBI to suppress this rebellion. Dickie Wilson was the questionably elected President and after 2 terms solidly controlled all aspects of the Reservation. I met some former GOONS who had changed their minds about this tragic period. One was planting a large garden at my friend's buffalo ranch. Leonard Peltier was part of the AIM (American Indian Movement) Lakota Oyate People's Defense. The day the FBI drove recklessly into the Jumping Bull compound The AIM members and local families were eating pancakes in a small house on a hill. Goons drove around the Rez randomly shooting into homes, hurting people and children.

Prayer during sweat lodge ceremony or Inipi in the Lakota language. Lodge is in background.

I have been in numerous sweat lodge ceremonies and I find them a real purification of body and soul. You never sweated like this before. Heat varies but can be so intense your abdomen aches. But no burning. It is pitch black inside except for the glowing hot stones. A person beats the drum and someone sings songs mostly in native language. I always learn something, have some type of personal revelation. Thoughts. We share our personal thoughts with the group and request prayers. I always look forward to them. The intensity of the heat clears away your external daily thought and then revelations enter your head. My lady friend, a doctor, said it was the hottest heat she had ever experienced. Afterwards we eat a feast together. I recommend this for everyone. Even presidents.

A LITTLE MORE ABOUT ME OUT THERE-

I often stayed in Rushville, NE. At one motel I talked with the lady owner on and on about the travails of the Lakota in the area and the local white's harsh treatment of them. A year later I called for a room and was turned down. I also became friends with two Lakota men when walking my dogs in the Park. I invited one to a steak dinner I grilled on my motel's picnic area. He didn't get much good food. He was considered by the town as a bum. This owner came out and sent us away. The next day he refused to rerent me my room, with the false excuse my dog had vomited in the room. See? As a white they really liked me and my business. Another time in Martin an old man with an arrest record was sentenced to 5 years in prison for stealing a loaf of bread. Of course, some whites and Lakota are friends and intermarry.

A phenomenon are the packs of REZ dogs. They are abandoned dogs who have also interbred. Not all feral, they are friendly and mostly skinny, bones sticking out. I also kept a 50-pound bag of dog food in my car to feed them. They ate in a fury of hunger. Some have the most distorted bodies you can imagine. Itz been said they sometimes take down a deer.

A friend was <u>June Little from Oglala.</u> He was very tall and skinny and wore his characteristic knee-high leather boots and had long flowing black hair with braids too. He was a civil rights full-blood who was a leader in the full blood takeover of the tribal administration building in 2000 protesting tribal financial corruption which caused shortages affecting parts of the tribe. They occupied the building for 11 months with no violence but the FBI was watching. I was the only white person who went in there to bring supplies and offer encouragement many times. It just hit me one day-help them out. I was inspired like that then. Some power had taken me over. The tribal meeting room was turned into a ceremonial meeting room. The tribal council held their meetings all over the Reservation at community centers during the Occupation. I remember sitting in the elected executive vice president's office talking to June as he relaxed at the VP's desk.

June showed me their plan for a new tribal organization based upon traditional Lakota values and asked me for my ideas. They were also demanding a forensic accounting audit of the tribe's finances. He lived there then in the office and slept on the beautiful leather couch. I was accepted by everyone. Eventually it ended. June died 10 years ago from throat cancer. He was a big smoker of unfiltered cigarettes. I met him the day I brought him and Tom Poor Bear of Wanbli, a pack of Camel cigarettes. They were surprised a stranger, a white, would show up and offer support of the tribes' protest of White Clay Nebraska liquor stores massive sales to the Lakota. They had a teepee encampment at the state border. Ten years later Tom was elected Executive Vice president of the Tribe. You can see the little modest poverty-stricken village of Wanbli in the movie Thunderheart. Let me say many of the leaders of the tribe are honest hard working and dedicated to helping the people. President Clinton visited in 1999 and created an Economic Empowerment Zone which had little impact.

Oglala Lakota College has an outstanding library and museum. All around the top of the walls are pictures of all the Reservation tribal presidents from 1876 to present. It amazed me at the changes in facial appearance and healthy vibrant appearance and firm confident expressions as time progressed and the Lakota declined and lost their way of life. They had shiny vibrant complexions and clear deep compassionate all-knowing eyes dressed in Lakota leather with colorful symbols and long hair. At time progresses complexions fade and become pale and grey, eyes lose vibrancy, and they wear white man's suits with short hair, faces getting full from being overweight. It is sad.

I was amazed to see young men <u>riding bareback</u> over the plains on typical <u>Indian Pinto horses</u> that we all have seen in the movies. That riding still goes on, it is strictly Indian, unchanged.

People tend to be quiet out there. My Indian students never much talked in class but were paying attention. In Lakota culture it is respectful to listen to elders, that is how you learn, not by interrupting and being loud. And elderly people are given utmost respect and still are leaders. Unlike modern societies.

Churches, churches, everywhere. Yep, the Christian religions really tried to civilize Indians and drive evil Indian Spirits out of them. To save them. Churches are everywhere. Even a Mormon church or temple. And there was competition for souls too. Today the churches do a lot of good. Red Cloud Indian School is a high performance Christian Catholic School providing a top-notch education and motivation. Many Lakota practice both their traditional ceremonies and beliefs and also Christianity.

The word TONKA means big, great, strong in Lakota. So remember those sturdy toy trucks and equipment models made in Minneapolis, Minnesota, call Tonka Toys? There you go, taken from the Sioux language.

The word Sioux comes from the northern Great Lakes Ojibwa Tribes' word which means "little snakes" The Ojibwa, (the Lakota, Nakota, and Dakota rivals) called them this because they wandered over the Plains following the buffalo in a zig zag. Imagine the overwhelming shock and fear of the Sioux tribes as they witnessed the mass slaughter and skinning of thousands of buffalo. The hides and skins were used for ornamental fashionable reasons to satisfy the vanity of European Whites. And for profits by the killers (not hunters), skinners, and middlemen who sold these valuable commodities. And to think the Indians only used the buffalo for survival, for food, teepees, and clothing, blankets. They didn't make one red cent. The US government approved a policy to kill off all the buffalo to subdue the rebellious Plain's Indians and make them prisoners, or pitiful wards of the US. It worked.

And to think the US minted a coin, the highly admired and collected Buffalo Head nickel. I had a few. When the summer tourists visit Yellowstone Park and places with Buffalo, I hope you can remember this horrible history. Hey, by the way, do you think this fits the definition of "Genocide"? This might be the only example of the entire population of an entire continent being destroyed and subjugated. Oh, and the wolves experienced the same thing, to please ranchers, farmers, and provide warm fashionable winter clothing. 1,000,0000 wolves murdered in the USA by 1900. About the same time the Buffalo were eradicated. This also was a US Government policy. This is wildlife Genocide.

The University of New Mexico should not be permitted to use the word LOBO (means Mexican Wolf) until it takes a political stand to save this species which is down to about 88 wolves and is endangered. Most students, professors don't even know this terrible situation. The LOBO statue on the campus should be covered over by canvas. The university should begin an education program and have displays around the campus especially at the sporting arena where many fans can be educated. There should be an official WOLF LOBO DAY sponsored by the school. This won't happen because the University Board is afraid of losing State funding or offending important people. And University of Colorado Buffaloes, with your mascot, the huge live Buffalo named Ralphie, the same goes for you. Using these mascots without historical education of their horrors is just exploitation of the animal, pure and simple, no different than the mass killings in the past. Does anyone disagree with me? C'mon explain it. It's not funny.

Billy Mills, a great (TONKA) man and Olympic Gold Medal 10,000-meter long distance champion and World Record Holder in 1964 for the USA. Read his book, Running Brave, and see the movie. He founded Running Strong for Indian Youth, an organization to help Indian youth. He travels extensively making talks to promote Indian pride and, promote healthy lifestyles and success. Like me, he became an alcoholic when he quit running, and recovered. He now leads a wonderful exemplary life and helps teach to eradicate the Native American scourge of alcoholism. He became a successful life insurance representative by selling life insurance and other financial saving products to the Indian people to help future generations move out of poverty. He also speaks to corporations about what success means. He has a very soft spoken warm voice and presentation. I have his video and show it to my college classes about being an American Indian businessman and using traditional Lakota values to improve and moderate capitalism that overemphasizes winning, money, and domination. It pertains to anyone. I have great admiration for him.

The Seven Lakota Traditional Values given by the White Buffalo Calf Woman are Praying, Respect, Caring, Compassion, Truth, Generosity, Humility, and Wisdom.

I forgot to tell you about the "Giveaway" (Wopila Ceremony) when Indian people achieve success or an honor or a birthday or anniversary, unlike all of us, they do not receive gifts, but give presents away! They honor their supporters. I have been to one and received a gift. This was the first-year anniversary of a woman's husband's death. In the Lakota Way, a bereaved person is allowed, or encouraged to mourn and grieve for one year. They take a year off from normal routines. But at the end of one year it is time to get back to living a good happy life. There is a celebration and a giveaway.

It is great to have money so you can give some of it away. Once I met a poverty-stricken couple at Wounded Knee. The young man, age 23, was a traditionalist that wanted to struggle for his people, the Lakota, for their civil rights, pride, living standards, and freedom. I had money then, so I pulled out a Ben Franklin, or a $100 bill and just gave it to him. He was not asking for money. He was so surprised, happy, and grateful. So was I. And it created a connection between us and a positive event between two races and former strangers.

One of my Step-Dad's best friends, Dick Fiscella, told me when he was about 88, the best thing you can do to lead a good life is to do one act of extra kindness a day. Good thing he was also a political member of the Democrat Party! Let me tell you something. He told me about the same time about WWII. He was a US Army Intelligence Officer Captain fighting in the Pacific at Iwo Jimo and Okinawa in 1945. He was assigned a Japanese interpreter, a guard, and a flamethrower specialist. His job was to locate enemy soldiers hiding in the many caves and coax them out to surrender safely. But, if they resisted the soldiers were blasted and burned to death alive. Those were his orders. These encounters are on TV on WWII documentaries. He said he never thought about it until a few years ago when the memories came floating back. He would just break up and weep and cry from time to time. War kills everyone, even if we don't know it. After the War he became an accountant and stayed in the US Army Reserve and reached the rank of a full Colonel. He is from Oak Lawn, Illinois.

One of the things that can be done is to create a revival and reconstruction program funded by the Federal Government. It would be very expensive and require reducing some current national programs or raising taxes. This would cost billions of dollars and is never going to happen. Most Indian programs are underfunded. Most federal benefits and eligibility are the same as non-reservation Americans. Since most reservation Indians are in poverty or disabled the Reservation has become what appears to be a welfare state. The only treaty benefit remaining is the Indian Health Service. Social problems are severe since tribes had their traditional way of life upended and fell into a long-term generational poverty trap. The isolation of Reservation areas also contributes to this cycle. In the 1950's the US tried to urbanize Indians and literally forced many to relocate to cities like Los Angeles, Chicago, Denver. That had limited success but it was a form of cultural destruction. Many could not adapt and returned to homes on the reservation or became trapped into poverty in big cities.

The one thing you notice on reservations is the lack of recreational facilities except for high schools. There are almost no parks, hiking trails, public swimming poos, tennis courts, golf courses, or indoor recreational centers. There is little interest in recreational healthy exercise. No social centers. People do not lift weights or do yoga and group exercise programs. This needs improvement. There needs to be many social workers and recreational staff assigned all over the reservation. Swimming pools and parks and athletic fields are necessary to improve health, lower social issues, crime, and make people more productive. More housing units need to be built and upgraded. Public transportation

needs to be provided. Schools need professional tutors. There are not enough jobs, but economic development projects seem to not work well, except casinos, and most tribes do not have high enough revenues from them to provide all these improvements. A few small tribes near big cities are very wealthy and people then incorrectly assume all tribes have plenty of funds. Not true. My guess is that the Pine Ridge Lakota Sioux tribal budget is $150 million, almost all federal money.

The reservation is a cash economy. Very few people have checking accounts. Almost everything is paid for by cash and money orders. The post office becomes a bank. Very few banks are on reservations. Because of this Indian family group culture, it is expected that you help others. Often a loan turns into a gift. People tend to be not adept at managing money and interacting with the commercial economy system. Once I bought a friend a $3000 pickup truck he really needed, although I had second thoughts about this as being too generous. Two months later I returned and asked how he liked the truck. His 20-year-old nephew and his unmarried "wife" needed the truck to visit her family in Oklahoma so he let them use the truck. Well something happened, and the truck disappeared down there. I was shocked, upset, and disillusioned. My best guess is that the nephew got stopped for speeding or had an accident, did not have insurance, and the registration was not in his name. The car probably got impounded by the police and the nephew and wife just left and returned to Pine Ridge, having almost no money and not understanding how to manage the legal system. Goodbye car.

But money is in short supply. It was not uncommon for me to provide gas money. Often about three weeks into the month people run short of money and food and ration carefully until the next month arrives and their checks.

The Naïve American traditional concept of wealth means one had lived well, been responsible and sufficiently skilled. One had done good and had enough resources to give some away to gain respect. Power and wealth were gifts from the universal spirit and related to all existence of mother earth. This was viewed as a threat to mainstream society. In 1922 the US Indian policy as stated by the Federal Indian Commissioner Charles Burke was to foster a competitive, individualistic economy and a Christian faith using missionaries as aides. The concept of "Giveaway" is a form of communal socialism and essentially income redistribution. As I have experienced and stated the Indian culture is at its roots socialistic and not capitalistic. Status was achieved by giving away much of your wealth.

The people are strongly connected to their homeland and many do not want to leave it. Interestingly, there is still some nomadic tendencies, as people come and go from the Rez to work, or visit and stay with relatives, without a strict schedule. That is why the US Census count underestimates tribal populations. And as in underdeveloped countries around the world the average age is very low. Much of the population is under 18. The median age in the US and Europe is about 36. On the Rez 25 years. The high school drop out rate is 71%, and 28% of the population has a high school degree.

I recently met a brother and sister, middle aged, in the park where I run. Turns out both are Lakota Sioux Indians from the Rosebud Reservation in South Dakota visiting relatives. And guess what!

Randolph ran a 4:17 mile and 9:23 two mile in high school, outstanding performances. He didn't continue running nor go to college which is typical on the Rez. His sister was heading to Flagstaff, Arizona soon to visit a friend for some indeterminate time after visiting her son in Albuquerque. Randolph had a severe case of diabetes. He had a terrible motorcycle accident this year in South Dakota and lost one leg below the knee and the front foot of his other leg, so he had difficulty walking. Both lived off of social security disability payments and some federal benefits back on the Reservation. They spoke in an accent that made it a little difficult for me to understand them. I bought them some food and sodas at a local convenient store. Then I dropped them off at a shaded area near the apartment complex, but it was an open area next to a dirt road where they hung out close to the apartment complex where their relative lived. All seemed typical to me. She was a runner and had finished a workout in her neat jogging outfit. That is good. I would like to talk with them again.

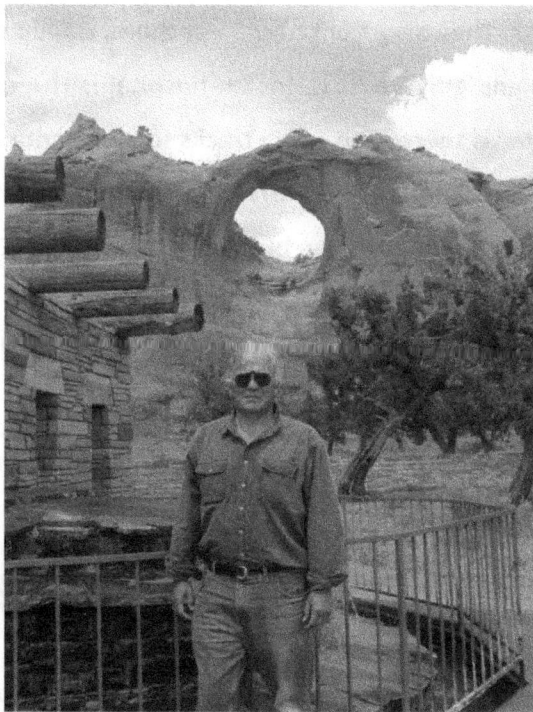

Window Rock 2009

NAVAJO PEOPLE –DINE'

I worked and lived on the Navajo Reservation for one year, 2008-2009. It was different there than Pine Ridge. I experienced some different interesting things.

Once a day in the mornings an old Navajo woman would walk her herd of sheep and goats by my apartment hogan near the college. She was dressed in a colorful dress down to her ankles, wore a scarf over her head, and carried a walking stick or staff.

Teachers lived in their own little detached brick apartments shaped like a traditional Navajo hogan with 8 sides. I mostly kept warm with a very hot wood burning stove besides gas heat. In the mornings in February the morning temperature was sometimes 4 degrees F. but by midday was 33-37 F.

Tsaile is about 75 miles south of the Utah border and 10 miles west of New Mexico. Running near it are the isolated 10,000-foot Chuska mountain range. The little town is at 7200-foot altitude. It has scrub trees and Ponderosa pines as you go one mile east towards the mountains. It is an 85-mile ride south to Gallup, New Mexico. Dine' College, where I taught, is located in Tsaile.

I went to Gallup about every two weeks on Saturday and Sunday for a change of pace and to eat a good meal in a nice sit-down restaurant. I stayed at the Red Roof Inn with my two dachshund dogs and walked them in a couple of small desert parks. They also went to the Vet there. Gallup is mostly a white border town with many Indians that come and go. The large Indian hospital is there. There is a decent golf course. A gigantic rail switching center is there with many tracks for the Santa Fe-Burlington Northern freight trains. There also many Indian jewelry and art stores mostly run by whites who buy Indian art. They cater to tourists mostly. The town is alongside the busy interstate Route 55. There are a few small patches of the extended Navajo Rez alongside the town in stark contrast to the middle-class housing in town. I did major food shopping on Sunday at the local Walmart. It was jammed, mostly Indians. Gallup has by far the highest crime rate in New Mexico and the country. Much is petty crime like theft, disorderly conduct, fights, but also some murders. Outside the town and heading 50 miles north is the beautiful red rock country.

A large herd of sheep and goats roam the college grounds. Maybe 50. Sometimes they blocked the door out of the school.

There are NO fences on the Rez anywhere. All animals roam free including horses and cattle. Mostly small groups. In the morning I would find fresh cow pies around my place. Other times they ate scrub grass outside my place. Once a steer bumped my window door frightening me. I hid behind the couch afraid he might break in. A family of five horses used to come and go from their owner's barn a mile away. The small young colt used to romp and play, kicking his hind legs way up behind him. Neat. There was a trail they would trot single file back and forth. One time I was running on it and here they came, 5 in a row. I had to jump aside. They had instincts and cohesiveness. A good life.

Outside my back door one spring a small wasp nest appeared. I let it grow for 5 months. I never used the door. It grew bigger and bigger, more wasps. They sleep huddled together on the outside of the hives. Once I saw a big one try to lift a dead caterpillar to try and fly it back to the nest for a big dinner for everyone. I noticed a chunk of the caterpillar's back was bitten and missing. The wasp had taken a bite. They eat other insects. I learned something from these little scary guys.

Navajo woman tending sheep and goats. Roamed the campus and teacher housing area

Me and my best friend Pi. I miss him.

The neighbor teacher's dog adopted me. He used to wait for me. I played with him and gave him food and water. Once in the morning I went to the front door and there he was patiently waiting for me. He also had a friend dog who hung out with us. He limped because his owner had kicked him hard. We were brothers, for real. I miss them sometimes. We connected, formed a bond.

I saw some snakes and eagles.

My neighbor Navajo Indian friend believed in skin walkers, evil like scary spirits, who cause or break curses. Transform into half human like animals at night, run as fast as cars., leave scratches on car doors. Many still believe. But in our reality, there are medicine men skin walkers who wear animal skins and have night ceremonies around bonfires. They live alone in remote places. I was told don't talk about them, because you will attract them.

The Reservation looked in much better condition than Pine Ridge, and people healthier.

It is the largest Reservation in USA. 27,000 square miles. 140 miles by 200 miles, the size of northern Illinois or from Chicago to Quad cities and from the Wisconsin border to Peoria. Or the size of New Hampshire, Vermont and Massachusetts combined. No telephone service to 80% of the land. Enrollment 300,000 with 250,000 on the Reservation, average age is young at 24 years, 170,000 speak Navajo and 186,000 are full blood which are very high numbers, unemployment rate is 49%.

I met Harry Chimoni at the Zuni Reservation in 2002. We hit it off and he though I was Lakota. He is a Kachina dancer and spirit man. He invited me to go along on the annual house to house blessing walk. Zunis have kilns in the back yard to bake bread.

I went to a Kachina harvest ceremony on the Hopi Reservation. This was a soulful

almost primeval dance with drums and chanting in perfect rhythm. I must go again. A connection to the earth and universe. No cameras. On second Mesa. The Hopi are very spiritual with strong unchanged traditions and a connection to the Natural Way. Many ancient predictions happened. Such as man would ride on a cloud near the ground (cars). There would be cobwebs in the sky (cell phones, TV, radio, satellites). From hundreds of years past. Also their ET connections.

People on First Mesa live as in past, no utilities, no electricity. They have a rattlesnake handler ceremony and dance.

It is Ok to go to any Rez alone without knowing anyone in advance or why you are there. Something always happens. Just go along, it will find you. What you need, who you are.

Navajo people are properly called Dine' (Duhnaa) in their language

Much uranium mining was done on the Reservation. Cancer rates high. Tribe has banned all mining. Around borders of Rez drilling and mining is springing up .

Navajo spiritual practice is about is about balance and harmony to a person's life based on Hozhoojf. Must maintain balance between man and Mother earth. Perimeter of their land has 4 sacred mountains, one on each corner. I want to hike Mt. Taylor at Grants New Mexico, a massive extinct volcano. Very large rattlesnakes are in this remote area.

Monument Valley is on the Navajo Rez in Utah, beautiful and pre-historic. Site of many western movies.

When I was in wandering from place to place in Pine Ridge all those years no harm ever came to me. So forget the itinerary, just go.

The Original Pull to the Pine Ridge Experience 1996-2008

Here is how it started. I was at home in the yard, alone, my wife had long gone, and career ending harshly, and reconsidering my life and its purpose. I had a feeling something was pulling me in west by northwest direction, which on the map goes directly through southwestern South Dakota and Pine Ridge. I said to myself, "something is out there". That summer I met all sorts of local people in Chicago and went to Indian activities. Each meeting opened up another door and passageway. My friend and I had heard about two more white sacred buffalo being born out there and were invited by Floyd Hand, so off we went. I had some unusual thoughts and dreams. I had a premonition and a vision that there was a vortex out there I had to find. I had had a sitting with the Mitchell-Hodges mysterious powerful crystal skull uncovered in Central America in 1925. Some had said extra-terrestrials had created it, others believed it was a spiritual connection to the unknown. I touched it with my three middle right fingers and a rainbow appeared inside it, which shocked the owner who was traveling around the USA to various exhibitions. I drove all over the Rez in a certain area, got maps from the BIA, and tried to figure this out. The touched fingers also were like GPS guides. I had some more revelations in an intense Inipi or sweat lodge ceremony. The last day I was there I took a long walk down an isolated trail south of the Oglala Reservoir looking for a special spot I had visualized with a small pine tree in an open area that had some connection to me. It was late in the afternoon so after one mile I was about to give up when I decided to walk a little further over a small hill on the trail. At the top there it was, a small pine tree out in the open. I walked down and around and smelled the strong beautiful aroma of pine. And what did I find? There was a circular sun dance area. This a sacred ceremonial place which connects the spirits of men and the earth with the Great Spirit. In essence it is a spiritual vortex, a spinning tornado like an invisible spiritual power that people encircle and pray. I had found the vortex! I was stunned. How could I know about this I asked myself? I headed back and had picked up a long branch for a walking stick. On the way a thought struck me that a man and his dog would be standing by my parked car. And sure enough, there was a man with his dog waiting for me to ask why I was there. And I had a big bag of dog cookies in the back seat, so I gave his dog a handful. Strange silly? But I had known about this in advance. This is only part of the big story. I was changed for life.

ED HIGHBEAR CHEYENNE RIVER RESERVATION

My good friend who died of bone cancer at age 62.

READERS NOTES: Do you realize many Indian Reservations are very different places that mainstream USA or Europe? Life has a different pace, and in some ways a trip back in time.

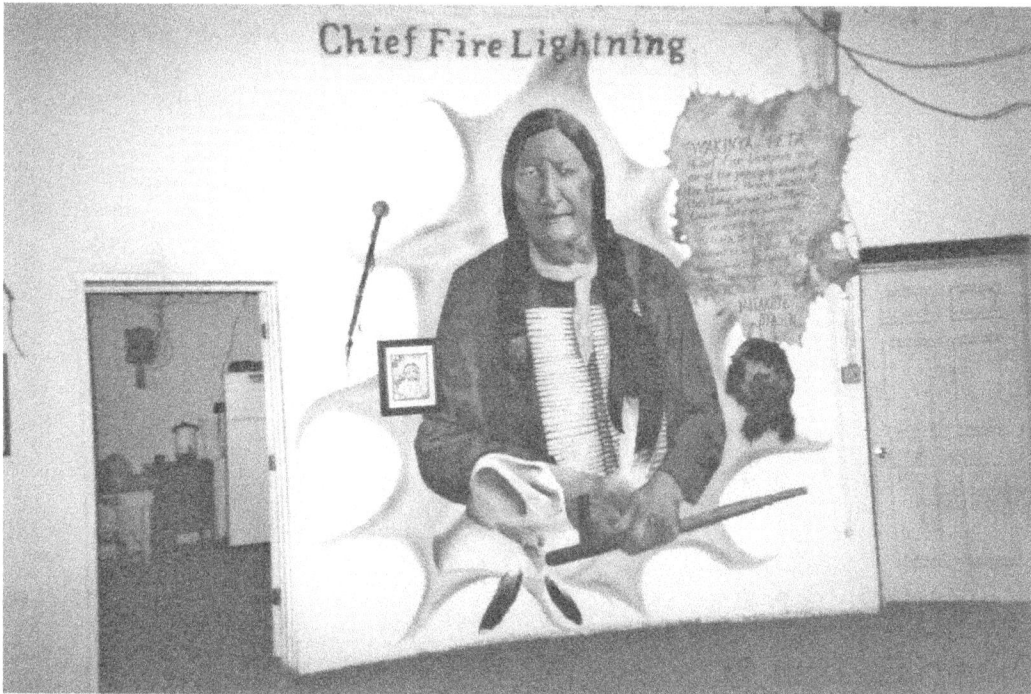

Wounded Knee Museum Chief Fire Lightening

Little Girl in Village of Green Grass on Cheyenne River Reservation-an isolated area. Arvol Looking Horse Keeper of the Sacred Lakota Pipe "Chanupa" lives in Green Grass

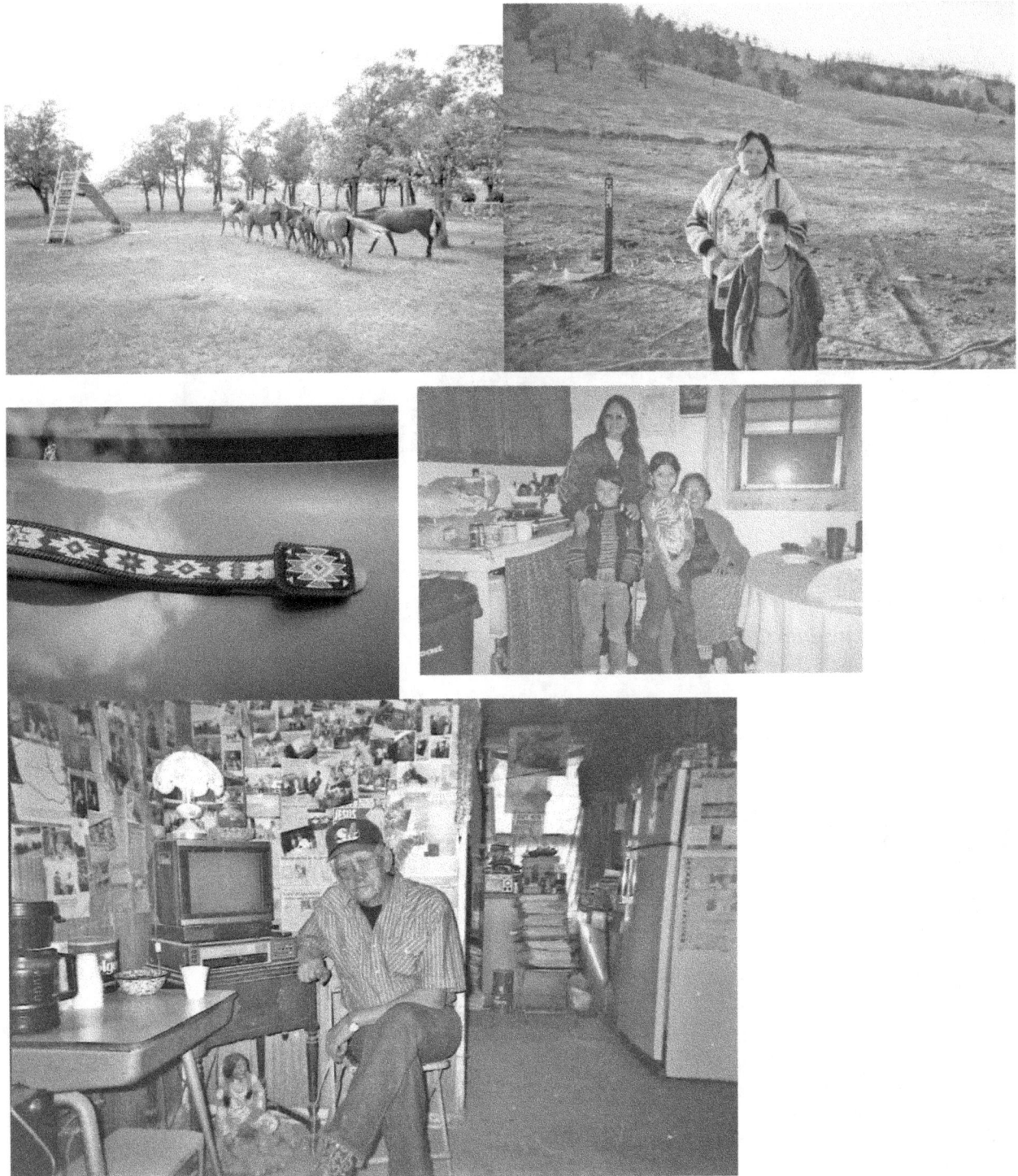

Tony "Buzzie" Blackfeather--Lakota Rights Leader

Other pictures above left to right above: Resident horses in Green Grass roam free; Marlene Locke from Porcupine South Dakota and grandson; belt made by Richard Grass; Grandmother Lydia, Norma and children at home in Wounded Knee.

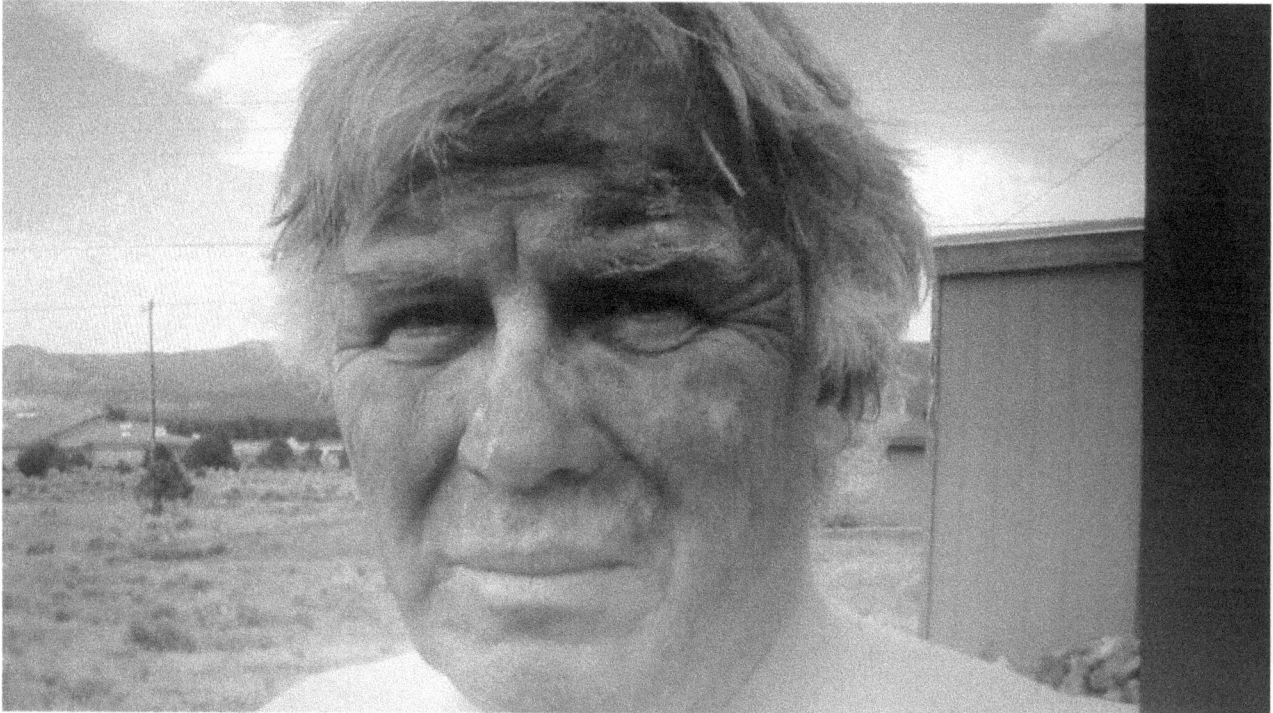

Me gone ROGUE on Navajo Reservation 2008-wild out there Lots of Laughs

THE GERMANS: By the way there is a large following of Native Americans in Germany. They have built Indian villages and have various organized groups studying history and culture. Many visit Indian Reservations each summer here in America. One such group is the Native American Association of Germany e.V. or NAAoG e.V.   **Contact:** chairwoman@naaog.de **(in Germany)**

Vice-Chairwoman-G.Yellowhorse@naaog.de **(in USA)**

SIOUX WAR CLUB

CHIEF SITTING BULL

He was not a war chief but a leader and spiritual man. Before the Battle of Little Big Horn he did a vision quest in which he put numerous cuts into his arms, one by one gradually over 2 days, without food or water, totally immersed in prayer. His vision was accurate and uncanny. Before the 7rth Cavalry soldiers had arrived, he saw many of them falling into the Lakota encampment, on their horses. This is what happened two days later as the soldiers attacked down the Big Horn Creek and from the top of a nearby hill. The soldiers were repelled and attacked. The Lakota have always been very proud of this victory.

My friend Joe Bear Cloud member of Crow Tribe by Battle of Little Big Horn Store

Friends home Porcupine Community at Pine Ridge. Seven people live there

I have to say this about the Indian People, they saved me. I mean I was kinda lost and in pain over my divorce and the ending of my banking career. Those people gave me a purpose and showed me another world, a different way of thinking and looking at the world. A genuine kindness, respect, and humility, and a great sense of humor. Enjoying life without a lot of stuff. I never regret the years I was among them. Most of you will never experience this great culture the way I did. To me it is worth gold.

Muori Minoto-<u>Kenyan boy.</u> I sponsored Muori through the Children's Christian Fund. For several years I sent money and we corresponded from age 12-16. I have a stack of letters an artwork he sent me. He was very garteful for all that I sent him and always said God Bless You. He bought a knit polo short sleeve shirt and khaki pants for school and said he looked very snazzy. His father was very grateful he could buy goat meat one time for the family. He also planted an orange tree with my name on a sign below it. He also bought a corrugated metal tiny house for himself and his girlfriend. I was always touched by Muori and still miss him. Unfortunately, the Christian Children's Group broke all contact off with him when he reached 18. I called the headquarters in Virginia but no luck. This was their policy. Cruel I thought. They sent me another boy, a wonderful Ugandan, but I turned them down. I had done enough. I wonder about Muori. He must be about 30 years. I have his picture.

Living in Chicago-the Spirit Stuff

A couple of other things. In the 1980's I became a very strong fundamental Christian. I joined a new church started by a recent Moody Bible institute graduate. It inspired me, and I made some great friends. This was in Lisle and Naperville, Illinois. I read most of the Old Testament page by page and studied much of the New Testament. I was deep into a spiritual connection. I also had some big post-divorce issues about child visitation with my two young daughters, then ages 10 and 13. One morning I woke up and was feeling anxious and sad about the divorce mess and missing my kids and whoosh! A powerful feeling and sound like rushing wind went into one ear and out the other for about 5 seconds. I was fully awake. And all the anxiety and sadness just left me. I was content all day and couldn't even make myself unhappy. This happened another time too. I always wonder about this.

Alcoholism----After I graduated from college I steadily drank more and more and became a businessman alcoholic. In other words, I could function, hold a job, but my drinking got worse as the years passed on. In those days drinking with customers and business parties was commonplace. By the time I reached 40 years, heavy bouts of drinking in bars, parties, and alone at home were commonplace. I am lucky I was never in an accident nor arrested.

I thought life would be so dull without drinking, how could anyone do without it and enjoy oneself.

I got a new great job and finally was determined to stop. I didn't want to make a fool of myself at office parties or come to work late and hungover. So I went to Alcoholics Anonymous. I remember being at my office about 6 PM waiting to leave for the first meeting nearby at 7. The office was empty. I looked out my expansive office window at the beautifully landscaped office grounds and said a little prayer for help. Tears came into my eyes. And off I went to the meeting. To me a miracle happened. The urge to drink just vanished. I didn't even sip a drink for 7 years! How could this be? I went to many good AA meetings, but I had no struggle like other people. It was so easy. Some people thought I was not even a drinker, but just came to the meetings and made up my drinking stories. By 1998 I began very light occasional drinks, as I do now. I never slipped up. I have never been drunk, out of control, or had a hangover for 27 years. And I have had my share of problems. I love being clear headed.

About 2004 I also visited two local Chicago Orthodox churches that had statues of the Virgin Mary which were weeping. This was in the Chicago news. There, close up, I saw tear lines running down the bodies from their eyes onto a cluster of cotton balls at their feet. Is that amazing or what? Fact or fiction? I stopped by a beautiful Roman Catholic Cathedral like church on the south side near 53rd and just east of Ashland Avenue next to Sherman Park. It was a highly Polish ethnic neighborhood and a Catholic day of prayer on a Sunday afternoon. People were scattered about the church pews praying when I noticed a young woman on her knees praying and very slowly moving forward towards the church alter about 100 feet. What a sacrifice and strong belief to stay on your knees on that hard church marble floor. Just amazed me. That church has been torn down.

And one more animal experience-it's spiritual. I was at the Olympic National Park at Lake Quinault Lodge in Washington in 1999. I drove down a narrow road to a quiet isolated place in the forest about 5 miles from the lodge to experience nature. And two beautiful magnificent elk walked across the road into the forest and deep green ferns, so I followed them. I had to run and leap through the foliage to keep up with them. Suddenly, I came to a clearing, a big meadow, and right there was the herd, about 25 large elk. And then I saw the one male elk, standing guard over his females. He started doing the elk

clicking warning sound and seemed agitated, so I took off and headed back Now that was a thrill, I was so lucky. **AMAZING NORTHERN MINNESOTA WOLF PACK EXPERIENCE .FEBRUARY 2001 . I** was at a summer fishing lodge with the temperature 4 degrees. A few people were in cabins and eating meals in the main lodge, it was still open to unusual visitors. Dressed in 3 layers I drove down to a small roadside parking space and ventured down a snow covered narrow trail. After a while I came to an open area and to my amazement, I saw the snow imprints of 4 lunging wolfs! Fresh tracks of a chase. They went up a rocky snow covered hill but one turned left and went down the path 50 feet before taking a right into the rocky woods-the cutoff wolf to snare the deer. Another wolf track went further down the path for 200 feet until disappearing over a frozen like. Along the way were numerous scat and urine droppings. The pack was encircling the deer and this one was marking their territory. I went back 5 minutes later to the clearing and I heard the distinct yip yip yip excited cries of the wolves. They were celebrating their deer kill. And overhead Ravens were circling as they do in winter over wolf kills waiting to eat the remains. This is a way to find wolf packs. I was thrilled to be so close and a part of this natural event people rarely see. I felt blessed. I will never forget it.

<u>Conclusion:</u>   Well, it's been a long journey in this book for me, taking me back into the past. I hope you've enjoyed it. There are some other things, you know, I've discussed how I felt about it. I hope you learned about me a little and got a little extra insight into Lakota/Indian culture and life. So I hope you enjoyed it.

ALBUQUERQUE ROOSEVELT PARK

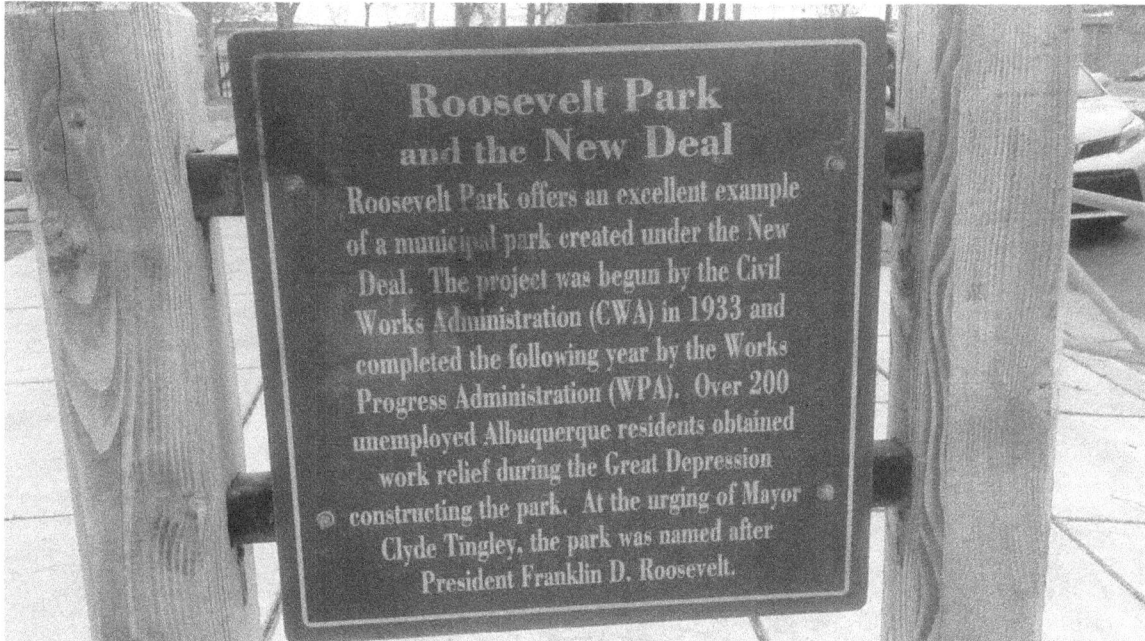

Roosevelt Park
and the New Deal

Roosevelt Park offers an excellent example of a municipal park created under the New Deal. The project was begun by the Civil Works Administration (CWA) in 1933 and completed the following year by the Works Progress Administration (WPA). Over 200 unemployed Albuquerque residents obtained work relief during the Great Depression constructing the park. At the urging of Mayor Clyde Tingley, the park was named after President Franklin D. Roosevelt.

BUILT IN ALBUQUERQUE 1935 BY 200 UNEMPLOYED MEN. WORKS PROGRESS ADMINISTRATION NATIONAL PROGRAM. THE PARK IS STILL USED TODAY 83 YARS LATER. IT HAS PROVIED MUCH PUBLIC BNEFITS. SOCIALIST PROGRAMS LIKE INDIAN CULTURAL ATTITUDES

LUNCH TIME at CCC or CIVILIAN CONSERVTION CORP. These 200 men did national soil, road, and forest restoration. Millions of trees were planted. The current National Park lodges were built. This is an example of tremendous public national benefits lasting until this day.

OLD GLORY USA FLAG

JACKSON PARK CHICAGO BUILT ON INDIAN LAND

CENTRAL NEW MEXICO COMMUNITY COLLEGE OR CNM

I have taught here for 9 years and it has been a great experience. I love interacting with the students and bringing the course work into current events and world trends. Economic trends and ideas are fascinating.

THE WOLVES

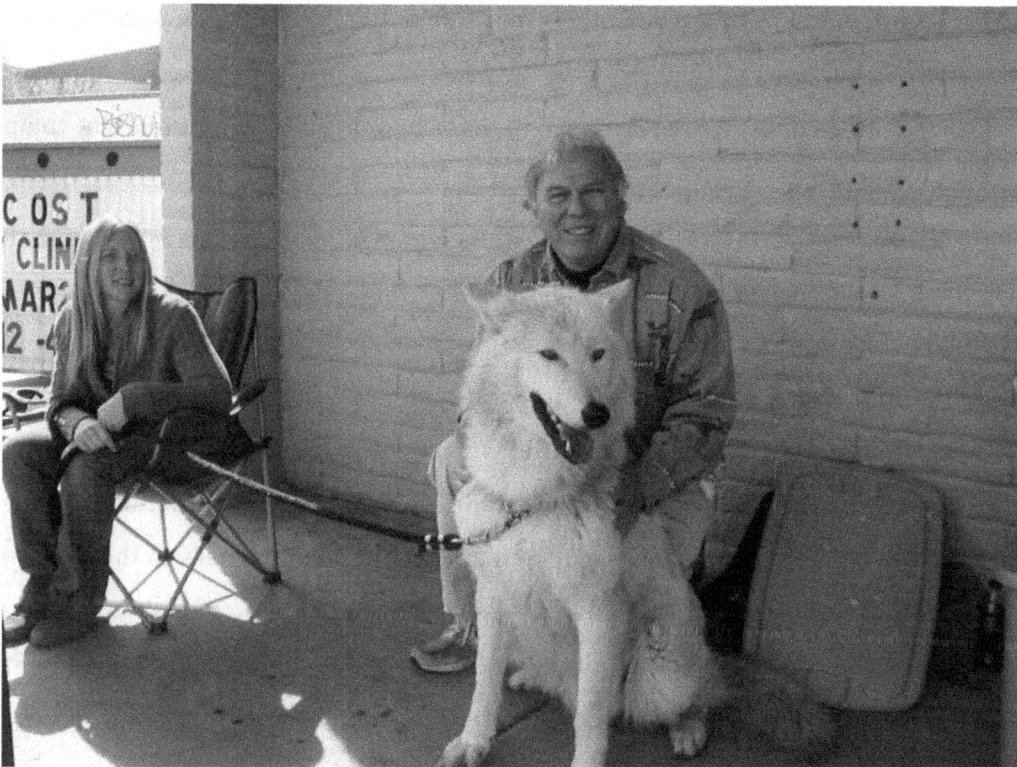

With the wolf Forest from Spirit Wolf Center

Yellowstone Park and the surrounding states of Montana, Idaho, and Wyoming had a large population of natural pure wolves, about 3500, with no cattle genetic material mixed into their wolf genes. Hunters and the State of Montana have recently killed about 1200. Some are trapped and die a slow tormenting death. Some pup dens are sprayed with poison gas. The wolves belong there but some ranchers aren't happy about that and they do very minor damage to livestock. Hey, who came first, the wolves or the ranchers and their cattle that alter the natural environment. Besides there is a federal wolf cattle compensation plan. The hunters are upset because without wolves the elk are easier to hunt and kill. The wolves keep the elk on their toes, alert, the herds are healthier, the wolves kill the older or weaker elk. Therefore, the elk are stronger, harder to track down. Like they are supposed to be as Mother Nature intended. And the original environment with bird and plant species is coming back. Some of these hunters lie and wait for wolves that are well known and very popular with tourists, and as they leave the edge of the park and boom, shoot them down, dead. One was named Blackie (a Black wolf, rare). These people hate the wolves and feel people are above them, and those states have the right to do as they please. Like Governor Butch Otter of Idaho who stated at a rally, "I want to be the first person to get a wolf killing license!!". (Idaho Press Tribune, idahopress.com, March 14, 2008). Governor Otto is a good man, well liked in Idaho. But he is misguided and insensitive to this sad wildlife killing. I'm sure they have some justification for this way of thinking, they always do. It is has to be stopped, this way of thinking. The wolves belong to all of us, we are connected, these people have no natural right to do this. And also to wolves anywhere in the USA, like New Mexico, Arizona, North Carolina, Wisconsin, Michigan, and Minnesota. This is no different than the horrific poaching of elephants and rhinos in Africa today. You think it can't happen here? By 1900 1 million wolves had been killed in the USA, about 99.9% of the population. What kind of crazy cold-hearted people could do such a thing? I encountered a wolf pack near Ely Minnesota hiking alone in the woods on a sunny 4-degree Fahrenheit day in February 2002. Just awesome. There are about 3000 natural wolves there too, in danger. Our former Minnesota Senator, my liberal champion, backed new legislation to ease hunting restrictions, I have been told and read. During the 2012 election wildlife wolf defenders sent 60,000 emails to the Obama Whitehouse asking him not to endorse new policies to ease regulations to hunt wolves around Yellowstone. A Senator from Montana, a Democrat, was in a close race for the Senate. So President Obama, and 2 powerful Senators, went to Mr. Salazar, Secretary of the Interior, to ask him to ease regulations and give the local states much more control over this issue. I have read this in a national wildlife organization article. There it is. I actually voiced my objection on the telephone to Secretary Salazar's assistant. The elite rule and ignore us when they want to get votes and get special favors. Zero tolerance on this issue. Now Congress is considering delisting the Wolf as an endangered species. A Native American Lakota friend of mine, Sam Red Feather, said they will delist the wolves from the endangered species so they can hunt and kill them, and then relist them when their numbers drop. Traditional Indians or Native Americans, as the mainstream society imposed this designation, are wise and see the world differently than the mainstream political society, thank goodness. Some people on this continent still have sense and compassion for wildlife. The Nez Perce Tribe in Idaho was key in reintroducing wolves into Idaho and watched over them. But the powers there went ahead and ignored this. These tribes are so beaten down and disrespected at times. Here in New Mexico the rare Mexican

Gray Wolf is almost extinct, with 113 in the wild, up from 62 over 5 years ago. The anti-wolf cattlemen's group is consistently trying to rid the area of wolves and is primarily responsible for poaching and killing wolves. They don't seem to think wolves have any intrinsic value and are a necessary part of the world. The University of New Mexico, their mascot The Lobo, should put up an exhibit in the student union and the basketball arena dedicated to the history and problems of the Mexican wolf.

PICTURES

Me and my Navajo dogs   University of Chicago, my school

Corporate Hog Confinement Pen

Iron Wood Pot Bellied Pig Sanctuary north of Tucson over 200 rescued-love this place!

Cattle around my Navajo teacher housing unit & horse family grazing near my house--No Fences on Reservation

BELOW: Lakota Ceremonial Feather-ABOVE: Elton 3 Stars relaxing in my Lazy Boy chair. He painted the pictures of the wolf and my 2 dogs in this book. They are lifelike, uncanny, you see and feel their souls, their essence.

Lakota prayer feather

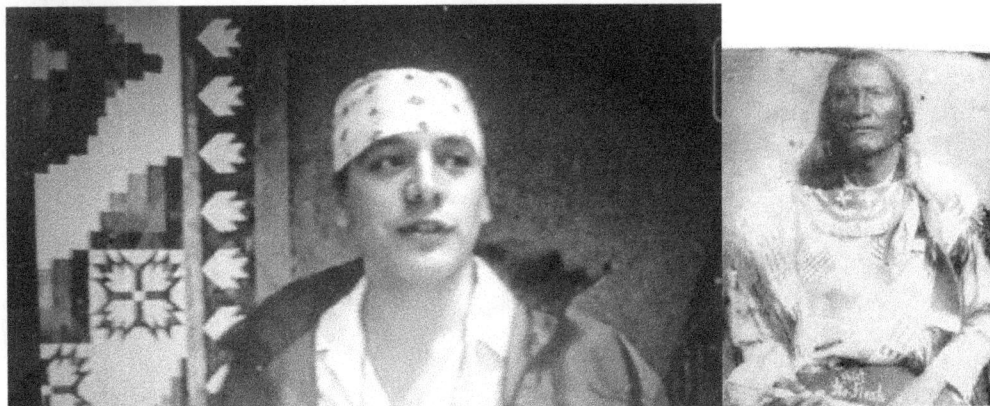

TOP: Marie Lange Lakota activist and friend; Gary Rowland and wife Lakota activists; Young Lakota man environmental activist. Chief Sitting Bull Lakota spiritual leader and wise elder 1876

Family at Chicago lakefront. Blaine, Brooke, John, Sarah, Katie

Above: Lakota friends

Me, Sarah, John, Brooke, the Grandchildren

Me and young students and teacher outside of Leningrad in 1968. This is about peace and the fact we are all one human race. I wonder what some of these little ones are doing today in Russia.

Carol Lakota friend. She has a carved non-ivory elephant collection

My dogs, Starstream (above) and Snugly (below). The greatest Dachshunds I've ever known.

Above: Merrillyn Sweet   Below: Lope and Pandi our friends. Soon to have their own children's book "The Adventures of Pandi and Lope"

Today 2019 at my park where I run 3 miles.

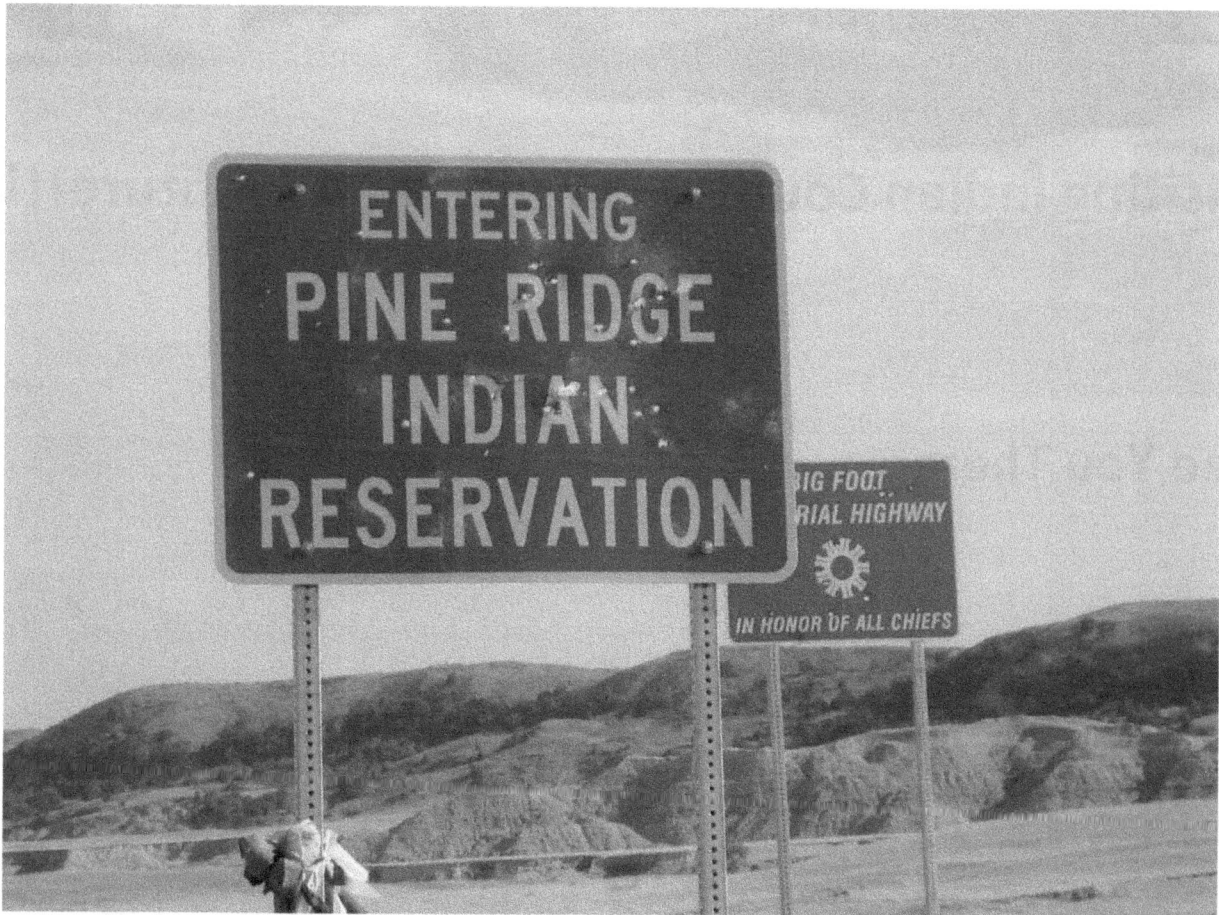

Not many people have been here or other remote Indian Reservations.

Pine Ridge Rolling Land

Visiting Indian Country is Quite an Adventure!!!

See You There

www.ingramcontent.com/pod-product-compliance
Lightning Source LLC
Chambersburg PA
CBHW080254030426
42334CB00023BA/2812